TODAY'S
TOMORROW

JOE ROBERT SURBER

TODAY'S TOMORROW

IMPROVING LIFE'S HABITS

TATE PUBLISHING
AND ENTERPRISES, LLC

Published by Tate Publishing & Enterprises, LLC
127 E. Trade Center Terrace | Mustang, Oklahoma 73064 USA
1.888.361.9473 | www.tatepublishing.com

Tate Publishing is committed to excellence in the publishing industry. The company reflects the philosophy established by the founders, based on Psalm 68:11,
"The Lord gave the word and great was the company of those who published it."

Book design copyright © 2014 by Tate Publishing, LLC. All rights reserved.
Cover design by Joel Uber
Interior design by Jomar Ouano

Published in the United States of America

ISBN: 978-1-62854-437-4
1. Body, Mind & Spirit / Inspiration & Personal Growth
2. Body, Mind & Spirit / General
13.11.11

DEDICATION

The writer is appreciative of the many good memories of his rather small family. This book is dedicated to his wife, Jody; his son and daughter-in-law, Robert Brian and Lynel, and his daughter and son-in-law, Karrie Jo and David Cuttler, and the writer's grandchildren, Jacob and Lydia Surber and Lexie and Sydney Cuttler. This book is also in memory of the author's parents, Hugh Richard and Dema Surber, and the author's brother, Hugh Richard (Dick) Surber.

ACKNOWLEDGMENTS

The author would like to express appreciation to the many individuals whose stories, quotations, examples, illustrations, or comments have been used in this book. Some of the information used came from college notes, minister sermons, guest lecturers, convention speakers, workshop presenters, newspapers, books, editorials, reviews, old textbooks, and radio and television programs. During some fifty years, the memories of who may have said what and when it was said have been intermingled or possibly attributed to the wrong person. In some instances, only partial information was recorded by or presented to the author. The author has attempted to acknowledge the proper individuals and portray correctly the quotations and information that is contained within this book. In particular, the author wishes to thank his former professors at Northeastern State University and Oklahoma State University for their instruction and guidance. Finally, the author wishes to acknowledge the mentoring of the deceased psychiatrist Dr. Edwin Fair, former director of the Bi-State Mental Health Foundation in Ponca City, Oklahoma.

CONTENTS

FOREWORD

We are changing every day. The direction, the extent, and the timing are mostly under our control. We are responsible for ourselves and for our behaviors, even though there may be unknown reasons for those behaviors. Much of our behavior results from habitual ways of behaving. If we repeat an action over and over, eventually it becomes a habit. There are some behaviorists who think that a habit occurs or develops when an action is repeated some twenty-seven to forty-two times. Most of us do not deliberately stop and think, *how do I tie my shoe?* We tie the shoe without thinking about it.

The 2012 book *The Power of Habit: Why We Do What We Do in Life and Business* by Charles Duhigg states that there are three steps in the process of developing a habit. I would add a fourth. I think that the four steps are (1) need or reason, (2) cue, (3) routine, and (4) reward. The last three steps are presented by Charles Duhigg.

An article in the March 4, 2012, *Tulsa World*, stated that a research study published in 2006 found that forty percent of our actions are habit, and no real decisions are made about what to do. The key thought to remember is that much of our behavior is without decision-making steps. This book gives encouragement, motivation, stories, and examples to help explain our thoughts and behaviors, and give insight into the decision-making process that allows us to change our bad habits. We can improve ourselves, and the later chapters of the book indicate how one can change a habit. Changing the habit often results in changing attitudes.

Certain habits, like drug usage, alcoholism, and most physical abuse behaviors are not helped by the habit-changing strategy and methods outlined in this book. However, we do have a number of other habits that can be changed by recognizing first that there is a need; secondly, making a decision to make the change; and finally, implementing the various steps.

We have to *believe* that *we can change*. We have *to want to change*. We have to *try to change*. We have to examine our habits that, in many instances, we use to excuse our behavior.

Former Secretary of State Henry Kissinger said, "Frequently, the perception of reality is more important than the truth of reality." What one believes to be so is more important than what is truthfully so. A very significant statement is made by Charles Duhigg in his 2012 book mentioned previously. He says, "This is the real power of habit: the insight that your habits are what you choose them to be." A very real problem is that most of us make many important decisions based upon emotion. As stated earlier, a research study published in

2006 said over forty percent of our actions are habits, with no real decisions made about them. Even when we think that we have given a decision careful thought, our reasoning may still be faulty.

David Kahneman, in his 2011 book titled *Thinking Fast and Slow,* states that even the smartest of us make flawed decisions. We are not even aware that we have made errors in our decisions. There are a number of reasons why we make errors in our thinking. Past experiences top the list, even though these experiences go through a filter that distorts the impression, sometimes significantly. During the 2012 presidential campaign, national columnist Bryon York said this: "And when something means so much to a group of people, they can easily convince themselves that it means that much to others, too."

There is some research on what is called *group think* that is prevalent among families, friends, and political parties. Habits evolving from early childhood rooted in group think can be tough roadblocks. Again, remember, recognition of problems must occur before solutions can be made. Awareness of the problem(s) is critical.

The next important element is the intensity or the strength of the need for a change. As rational humans, we need the comfort of coherence. We are influenced by what our friends or family believe, or what we frequently see advertised as true, or what we view on TV and what we read or see about our movie stars or sports heroes, or others who are important to us. Our emotions at the time of the decision can impact a decision. A daredevil or a cautious mood impacts a decision. The popularity (everyone likes...) of something often sways a decision. Commercials and media heroes guide many people's beliefs and behaviors.

One of the lesser known quotations is one from John Kenneth Galbraith, a former United States diplomat. He said, "Given the choice of changing one's mind or proving there is no need to do so, everyone gets busy on the proof." In a *Tulsa World* article dated March 22, 2012, whose headline was "Why Even the Smartest are Prone to Mistakes," the statement was made that individuals, "including scientists, often search for information that confirms their own beliefs." If wrong information or limited information is obtained, or if slanted information is inputted, then we have incorrect responses. Most of us are influenced significantly by our early experiences and our early-learned behaviors. Country or urban or inner-city environments often limit or significantly influence decisions, and thus the behaviors that result from those decisions. The music we like, the friends that we choose, the type(s) of entertainment we choose such as the TV shows that we watch or sports in which we participate or watch, our politics, and so on, *all* have some impact on the habits of behavior that we exhibit. We should remember that our behaviors are making memories for our families and our friends.

The good news is that we can change our behavior, and in changing our behavior, we can also change how we think and how we feel. We can control many behaviors, and in controlling the behaviors, we can then begin to control the feelings and thinking that initially set up the habitual behavior that is believed to be needed to change. As English writer James Allen (1864–1912) said of people in his short book *As a Man Thinketh*, "They themselves are makers of themselves."

In his book, some people believe that James Allen is thought to advance that there are two basic principles that direct a person's actions. A person is (1) today, where his thoughts have taken him, and, (2) he is the architect for his future, be it better or worse. A person goes from seeing (or hearing) things to knowing (or believing) things to doing (habits) things, all of which is surrounded by varying degrees of feelings. "Enthusiasm without knowledge is like running in the dark."—*Bits & Pieces* (1975). Intent is not enough, only a beginning. Finally, a final thought from a well-known writer from the past—a writer who mixed humor with common sense and a penetrating insight into human nature— Will Rogers is credited with saying, "Ignorance ain't the trouble in this world. Everybody knows plenty. It's what they know that *ain't so* that's the trouble."

SEVEN THOUGHTS TO ASSIST IN AVOIDING A WEAK BEGINNING FOR A YEAR'S SELF-IMPROVEMENT

Monday

Not everything that is faced can be changed, but nothing can be changed until it is faced.

—James Baldwin

Tuesday

Make it thy business to know thyself, which is the most difficult lesson in the world.

—Cervantes

Wednesday

To be what we are, and to become what we are capable of becoming is the only end in life.

—Robert Lewis Stevenson

Thursday

Of all knowledge, the wise and the good seek most to know themselves.

—Shakespeare

Friday

Have you examined your attitude about your situation? Your situation is often caused by your attitude.

—Leonard Andrews

Saturday

The human being does deliberately undertake, while reshaping the world, to reshape himself also.

—William Ernest Hocking

Sunday

He who stops being better, stops being good.

—Oliver Cromwell

INTRODUCTION

This book is designed to encourage the participant in a journey beginning with methods to recognize one's own strengths and weaknesses, and finishing with specific suggestions that help one to make life-changing behaviors. A person's behavior is a combination of thoughts, feelings, and actions. There are a number of excellent self-improvement books. What distinguishes this book from others is the use of illustrations, stories, quotations, common sense interpretations, and practical applications to known psychological principles. Except in extreme situations, a person is capable of improving and even radically and positively changing his or her behavior.

Each chapter is part of a system that ties together evolving concepts to develop self-realization and suggestions for self-improvement. The final chapters suggest a method for a major behavioral shift for the participant and should not be attempted until all of the earlier chapters are completed.

This book is not for the participant who has no need to change any behavior, nor is this book for the participant who thinks that he or she cannot change any behavior. The term *participant* is used deliberately, as the author believes that while he may make suggestions, any progress and improvement comes from actual participation and by practice by the individual.

A common theme is prevalent throughout the book. That theme is that the participant is able to make significant changes in his or her actions that can improve thoughts, feelings, attitudes, and behavior. Some participants will need to take more time and more practice, and for some, if true self-awareness is not accepted, any change may be impossible without professional help. This book will not help the participant who lives in a world of denial, the participant who is lazy and will not practice, and the participant who wants a quick fix to a problem that has evolved after years of development.

The participant must be willing to accept responsibility, must be able to accept an occasional mishap or a temporary loss of progress, and must believe that he or she is truly the master of one's fate. Reflecting on each chapter's contents stimulates the creative portions of the participant's mind and, in many instances, strengthens the desire to continue the positive improvement.

Finally, a person who has been physically injured may need qualified medical care; but if only bruised or scratched, the person may apply his or her own first aid. In a similar fashion, a drug addict would have need of professional help that this book is not able to make available, but this book would be of assistance

TODAY'S TOMORROW

for behavioral changes such as adjusting to a divorce or changing emotionally crippling perceptions of inadequacy.

Seeing oneself in a mirror is a sensory use of vision. Viewing oneself in an objective manner as seen in the mirror might be quite different. Perception, or the belief about how one looks "in the mirror" may be quite different than the image perceived by others looking at that person. It is the intent that this book will help a participant to perceive himself or herself in an objective manner so that any needed adjustments can be initiated.

If a person is hungry, he or she can make a meal or purchase one. A person may stay at home, go to a restaurant or a drive-in/out fast-food place. A number of factors determine the behavior to change the hungry feeling. Several things impact our perceptions and subsequent behaviors. For example, the intensity and the type of stimulus (seeing a bloody knife versus handling a bloody knife), the state of the sense that is receiving the stimulus (someone who must wear glasses trying to see something without them), or someone who has a hearing loss, or someone who is ill or distracted by environmental elements. Finally, the past memories and previous experiences all impact how individuals view the current situation.

Likewise, there are a number of self-improvement books. Some are more complicated, and other self-improvement books are very simple. This book attempts to be practical and is based on common sense and good psychological principles contained in very short chapters. There is purpose for every chapter that is useful in establishing a pattern for improving oneself.

A person's religious beliefs can be a source of comfort and strength. There are a number of excellent articles and books that offer insight and encouragement in changing a person's views and improving that person's behaviors. Some of the best books, besides the Bible, are those books written by individuals who have personal stories to relate. The common theme in all is that *doing* is the key to fulfilling the needs. Only a positive change in action can lead to the successful improvement of a person's behavior. Changing a person's thoughts and feelings are only a part of the journey. A person has to be patient and be persistent and, finally, must believe.

THE CHINESE COMPASS
(HOW TO MAKE THE BEST USE OF THIS BOOK)

There is an old saying that the Chinese have five points on their compass: There is north, south, east, west, and the point where the individual is now. A compass is used to give individuals a sense of direction. People must make the choice as to which direction they intend to go. They can decide north or south or east or west, or any point in between. The purpose of the compass is to guide them in the direction that they have chosen.

However, before a choice of direction is made and a determination to go, a person must first decide where he is. If a person is at point *A* and desires to go to point *B*, and point *B* is north of point *A*, then the compass provides him with the guidance (north) to reach his destination. However, if a person wants to go to point *B*, but he is unsure as to where he is, he does not know what direction in which he has to travel in order to reach point *B*. He must know where he is now before he can know in which direction he needs to go.

The purpose of this book is to provide some answers to several questions: Where are individuals in their journey in life? Do they have a clear sense of direction? Are they content with the way in which they behave? If self-improvement is needed, how can they take responsibility to improve their lives, and how do they become aware of what they need to do? And, finally, when do they begin to improve themselves?

The last question should be answered first. They need to begin today to improve themselves, not wait for tomorrow. Too many put off until tomorrow what needs to be done today. As for the other questions, this book is a beginner's compass for self-improvement and provides some answers. As the Chinese would say, "Once we know where we are, we know where we need to go."

Why do we wait until tomorrow to do what needs to be done today?

MIRROR OF MINE

In determining the direction of one's life, a number of people may justifiably ask the question, "Why should I change what I am doing?" or the question might be raised, "Why do others think that I need to improve?" There could be others who believe that their lives need to be enriched, or that there is something more to life than what they have already discovered.

If a person has a direction, where is the point of departure? It is difficult for everyone to see themselves as others see them. As Henry David Thoreau said, "It is as difficult to see oneself as it is to look backwards without turning around." To see oneself as others see him is similar to shaving with a razor without using a mirror. To see our face as others see our face, we must look into a mirror. We can use our eyes to look at our hands, arms and feet, but our eyes cannot see our face.

We use the same eyes, but as our face is too close to our eyes, we must look for a reflection. We can never see ourselves as others see us, for even a photograph is only a captured instant of what we looked like at that moment. All of us have heard comments like "this picture doesn't look like me" or "that's not a good photograph of me." The camera cannot reproduce what someone thinks that he or she looks like.

We must be able to assume that if people cannot see their face because their eyes are too close to their face, then people's behaviors cannot be seen objectively because their behavior is also too close. The behaviors are a natural part of themselves. As the eyes are too close to the face to see the face, the behaviors are also so much a natural part of the person that these behaviors, too, cannot be objectively observed by the person.

The term *mirror of mine* indicates a process that individuals should go through if self-improvement is a goal that is pursued through to completion. An individual needs to begin a critical self-assessment of improvements that he/she would like to make. The "mirror" could be comments from true friends and/ or sarcastic remarks made by hypocritical friends or enemies. If someone says, "Are you going on a diet?" or "Your trouble is that you talk too much," those are all the beginnings of a person's look into the mirror. How others may see a person may reveal unpleasant behaviors.

Many people may not like their looks when they peek into a bathroom mirror. Likewise, looking into a mirror of behaviors is sometimes unpleasant. But just as makeup can change a facial appearance, a change of behaviors can change a personality. Just as a person can use the mirror to see what he/she can do to make his/ her face more attractive or what needs to be done by someone else to make himself/herself more attractive, he/she can also use the mirror-of-mine concept to improve his/her behaviors.

As a wise man said, "At least some of our behaviors need to be improved so that we can like ourselves better and/or so that others may find our behaviors more attractive." He went on to say a critical thought: "Before we can change, we must know why. We must know where we are and where we should change."

A translation of the Scots poet Robert Burns may express this best:

> Would that some power the gift give us
> To see ourselves as others see us!

The mirror of mine is a primary tool to begin self-improvement. Unless we can see the bad habit or bad behavior clearly, without excusing or ignoring its consequences, we can make no progress in improving ourselves. The Foreword contained the information to explain why it is so hard to see ourselves as others see us. In the *Epistle of James* (kjv), the first chapter, it is said that when a man is a hearer and not a doer of the Word, he is like "a man beholding his natural face in a glass:" and then goes on his way, and "straightway forgetteth what manner of man he was." We look but we don't see, and too often we forget what we saw of ourselves that needed to be improved by change.

Why do we wait until tomorrow to do what needs to be done today?

WHY CHANGE A BEHAVIOR?

The question that a person may ask of himself or of another is "Why should I change my behavior?" or "Why is he/she attempting a behavioral 'facelift?'" For example, a decision to seek a divorce may raise questions about the behavior(s) that may have caused it.

There are several reasons for change. First of all, behavior is not static. Some change is inevitable, and then one must determine if he/she wishes to control the direction of change. Death is the only state of static behavior of any individual. Daily decisions impact the behavior of every person. Decisions will change a number of behaviors. Individuals determine the actions they take from the choices that are available. Never is there only one choice. The choices made point their lives in a direction that may be hard to change because of their habits of behavior.

Secondly, a person may be going through a recognized midlife reassessment of his/her purpose in life. As psychologist Dr. Carl Young indicates, the first half of one's life is directed towards achievement or obtaining material things. As a person enters the second half of life, there is more integrative approach

to life. Money, position, accomplishments, and other
material signs of success, while still desirable, appear
to be less important as one begins to search out the
meaning of the purpose of that person's life. People at
that stage look at the second half of life differently.

Some may feel the approach of their own mortality.
Others may feel like paying back or giving to a section
of society a portion of that which was given to them in
their climb to success. A person may say or think, "I am
in a position, either with time or with money, to assist
a cause or others, who need my help."

Behavioral psychologist Abraham Maslow
developed a need-hierarchy scale in which he stated
that until the lower need was satisfied, a person would
not attempt to satisfy the next need. For example, the
need for food and water (basic biological needs) has a
higher drive on the hierarchy then the need for safety.
Esteem needs are higher yet on the scale and do not
come into play until the lower needs are met. Maslow
also believed that a person begins to be more interested
and motivated to assist others about the mid-forties.
Most of the other basic needs would have been met
by that time, and the individual would turn to helping
others outside the family.

Finally, there may be a genuine feeling that one
can do better with his or her life. As the poet Henry
Wadsworth Longfellow said, "We judge ourselves by
what we feel capable of doing, while others judge us by
what we have already done!" Most biological scientists
and sociologists agree that motivation to change

appears to be an environmental and an inner biological or mental desire to excel.

Of course, there are other reasons to change one's behavior, but the three discussed above constitute the major reasons. A person's behaviors are a set of habits. Some of these habits may be self-destructive, either for that person or for others who are important to that person.

Before a person can take some meaningful action to change, he/she must ask the questions, "Why am I doing this?" and "How will I measure my progress?" and "How will I know that I have been successful in changing either a specific behavior or an interrelated pattern of behavior? Am I going to substitute a worse bad habit for the one that I am attempting to change?" As Aristotle said, "Excellence is not an art but a habit."

Why change a behavior? Because of a person's perceived need to do so! Success is dependent upon the awareness of the felt need, the initiation of the behavioral change, and then the constant practice of the changed behavior until it becomes a habit. Why change? Because of the need for improvement!

Why do we wait until tomorrow to do what needs to be done today?

TO BECOME WHAT WE WANT TO BE

A poem by John Masefield begins with these lines:

> There were three men
> Who went down the road
> As down the road went he.
> The man that they saw,
> The man that he was,
> And the man that he wanted to be.

What this writer was saying was that each of us are these three men, all wrapped up into one person. We are the person that others see; we are the person that only we know (as to what we are); but most importantly, we are also *the person that we can become.*

The person that others see us to be is not the complete person. If we know that we are being watched, our words and our actions are filtered so that most people see us acting out patterns of behavior. We try to project an image for others to see, sometimes to meet someone else's expectations.

The person that we really are is known only to us. All of us have had some past actions, thoughts, or feelings that we do not want anyone else to know. We many times know our weaknesses, if we have insight, but too many times we fail to know our strengths. A truly happy person must know himself as completely as possible and be satisfied with what he has made of himself. The key phrase is *what he has made of himself.* Only we are responsible for ourselves, not some external factor such as parents or society.

The third person then is the person whom we want to be. We are what we make of ourselves. We must have some goal to strive toward to give a sense of direction. We should be attempting to improve ourselves to be a better person. We can all become better spouses, parents, citizens, or workers. We can do more to help our fellow man in everyday activities as well as during the expected times such as Thanksgiving or Christmas or in times of crisis.

To become what we want to be may mean changing an occupation, a personality trait, or a false belief. To become what we may become may mean doing something for ourselves or, more importantly, doing something for someone else. We may develop or expand a philosophy of life, or a spiritual commitment, or improve our body or mind. In brief, to become the person that we want to be means to take action to improve and to fully expand our potential today and every day.

Why do we wait until tomorrow to do what needs to be done today?

THE BLINDERS WE WEAR

Philosophers have written about what is reality and what is truth. Why do we become blind to reality when we do not *want* to believe or see? We may "blind" ourselves to seeing things as they actually might be seen by most others. As the poet John Heywood put it,

> Who is so deaf or as blind as is he
> That willfully will neither hear nor sees?

A story is told about a mule named Jake who was exceptionally lazy. Jake would not work by himself, but if he were hitched up with another mule, Jake would work reasonably well. Jake probably figured that the other mule was doing most of the work.

The farmer sold Jake to an unsuspecting neighbor who wanted a mule for plowing his large garden. However, Jake would not work by himself. When the neighbor called the farmer, the farmer said that Jake was lonesome and would work only with another mule.

The resourceful neighbor thought of a method to trick Jake. He placed some six-inch squared pieces of leather on Jake's head harness so that Jake could only see straight ahead. A checkrein on either side kept Jake from swinging his head to either side to restrict his vision to the left or right. Jake couldn't see if another mule was by his side because of the blinders and the restricted range of motion when turning his head.

Jake was led into the traces and hooked up to the plow. The neighbor, out of sight of Jake, shook some chain and kept up a commentary about Pete's stubbornness and, in general, cussing all mules. The idea was that Jake would think that another mule was alongside him.

Jake fell for the trick. The neighbor used Jake for years, but Jake never saw "Pete, the other mule." The blinders placed on his head allowed him only to see straight ahead, and the checkreins kept his vision to a limited view.

While we can smile at the trick played on the crafty mule, we are victims ourselves of "blinders." We wear our own "mental blinders." How many times have we read of poets speaking of being blindly in love or being blind with greed, or being blind with anger or jealousy or envy? Our emotions place the mental blinders before our eyes. We are blinded by prejudice, love, and lack of experience. Our upset emotions provide us with our personal blinders.

Most of us are not aware that we are only seeing part of the picture or only seeing what we want to see. Unsuspecting, we wear our blinders in our daily lives. We sometimes treasure our blinders and resent someone else trying to tell us what really is. Years ago, speaking at a national meeting of the American Personnel and Guidance Association, Molly Vass from the University of Wyoming and Ed Jacobs of West Virginia University told the standing-room-only crowd that we all have "selective blinders." For example, they said, when a couple first meet, the individuals see what they want to see. Selective blinders may project an image of what they want to see instead of what really exists, may develop overgeneralizations, and may create absolute statements such as "We are made for each other." Selective blinders may also allow for input only of that information which only reinforces a comfortable or an emotionally charged belief.

The mental blinders we wear can become a convenient crutch. The mental blinders are also habit-forming. We must become aware of any blinders we wear. Only when we are aware of those blinders can we then take them off (if we desire to do so.)

Why do we wait until tomorrow to do what needs to be done today?

THE SPIDER MONKEY TRAP

Many of us have such a deep need for security that we trap ourselves in situations from which we could easily escape. We ourselves can escape from the security trap at any time, but we fail to see ourselves as being caught in the "spider monkey's trap."

The spider monkey is found in Central and South American jungles. The spider monkey has very long arms and legs, is very intelligent, and can jump up to thirty feet. Yet the spider monkey is one of the easiest monkeys to catch.

A hollowed-out container such as a coconut is used. A very small opening is made into the end of the hollow entrapment device that is chained or roped around the tree. Another larger opening on the opposite side is made. This is small enough that the spider monkey can only place his extended, slender wrist and fingers into the small opening.

Bait such as peanuts is placed within the hollow coconut. This otherwise intelligent monkey becomes trapped if he investigates the coconut and tries to get out the peanuts or other bait. The spider monkey traps himself. Once he puts his extended, slender fingers and wrist into the small opening and grasps the bait, his resultant fist is larger than the opening. When he tries to extract his clenched fist holding the bait, he cannot pull his hand out. By failing to release the bait, he traps himself.

Most of the monkeys remain caught in this simple trap until the trappers return. Even the danger of the trapper's arrival will not allow the wildly jumping spider monkey to let go of the peanuts. All the monkey has to do to escape is to let go of the peanuts and slip his hand out of the opening. Trappers have found the remains of a hand inside the coconut where a spider monkey had held onto the peanuts even when facing a tiger.

Many of us do not want to let go of the security we need and feel, even though we are trapping ourselves similar to the spider monkey. The monkey will not let go of the peanuts. We continue to hang onto the security of a known situation even though it might be bad for us.

Why do battered wives remain with the husband? Why does a husband remain with a job he hates? Who do teenagers jump at the chance to have a steady boy- or girlfriend? What holds teenage gangs together? The person's "security trap" is just as trapping as the coconut was for the South American spider monkey. The individual and the monkey both trap themselves.

Why do we wait until tomorrow to do what needs to be done today?

SEEING THE SAME DIFFERENTLY

We say we know that people see things differently; yet we find ourselves saying, "I don't know why he believes that," or "Why can't he see that doing this will cause him problems?" The question is, "Is the truth always self-evident?"

The illustration below demonstrates that different people can *look at, see* the same thing, and yet may arrive at different decisions as to *what was seen*. Many people may look at the illustration below and form an opinion as to what the illustration looks like to them.

Illustration 1

When they look again, they may not be sure that they see the same thing again. The principles of perceptual organization allows only one alternative view at a given time. It is either a white background or black, and once the background is set, then the figure emerges. There are at least two opinions as to what it looks like! This classic illustration by Edgar Rubin, an early 1900's Danish psychologist, is familiar to psychology students. Some people see only part of the illustration because of looking at only one part of the figure-background. One answer could be two profiles of black people looking at each other. Another answer could be a white vase on a dark background, or a third answer could be an upside-down, white Liberty Bell. Various people view the ambiguous figure-ground differently.

This simple visual illustration of people looking at the same illustration and not seeing all of the possible answers demonstrates part of the reasons for differing opinions. If people cannot look at this and agree what the illustration represents, think of the greater difficulty in reaching agreement on nonvisual situations.

Individuals have been heard to say, "Can't you see what will happen if you…?" What is perfectly clear to some may not be clear to someone else, as each may "see" something else, even though both are looking at the same situation.

We need to be aware that someone else may be sincere in saying that he sees a situation as being different. A more cautious response from our increased understanding of different views may avoid another's emotional response invoked by an abrupt, "You're wrong!" A better response could be "Have you thought of...?" or "Could the problem instead be...?" Others may see the same thing differently, and who is to say which is correct?

Why do we wait until tomorrow to do what needs to be done today?

I MYSELF CAUSE MYSELF

Most people like to take credit for their success and like to blame others for their failures. Also, most people have more failures than successes because of the manner in which a failure is determined. Many people would agree that "I myself cause myself to fail." Many would not.

Epictetus, a former Greek slave, said centuries ago that "I myself cause myself..." Even though a slave, he felt that he was a slave only if he thought of himself as a slave and accepted that condition. Epictetus also said, "It is not the event but my judgment of the event that causes me to be upset." Instead of allowing others to control his thinking and therefore his life because he was a slave, he exercised control of his mind and spirit. It is how one responds to the condition of life that determines if one is a slave to others' commands or responses, or if one is master of his own future.

Blaming one's misfortunes on others is a mental drug that could be more deadly than a physical drug dependency on narcotics or alcohol. In most instances, the individual falls victim to blaming of others for his lack of success first, and then turns to the narcotic influence of "wish fulfillment" and escape of reality. If one can blame others for his failures, it is easier to blame others for his drug dependency. In both instances, the individuals are wrong.

The establishment does not keep someone from becoming successful in a career or in some financial endeavor. It is easy to blame the office holders, the "up owners," Wall Street, the governments, segregations or racial prejudice, living on the wrong side of the tracks, parents, education, etc., for one's own lack of motivation or work ethic or courage.

How can a person be successful if he thinks of himself as a failure? In the Bible it states "as a man thinketh in his heart, so he is." Writer James Allen, in his book *As a Man Thinketh*, said, "As he thinks, so he is; as he continues to think, so he remains." He believed that "a man is literally what he thinks." If a man thinks that others control his future, then he begins to live under that control. He allows others to control his life because he thinks that they must already do so.

A person, then, causes himself to be either successful or a failure. Assuming responsibility for changes is the first step to improvement and, along with awareness, provides the impetus for self-direction.

Why do we wait until tomorrow to do what needs to be done today?

THE SUNGLASSES ATTITUDE

A writer once said that "some people see evil wherever they look!" This is another way of saying that people see what they expect to see, and what is seen may not be as things really are. There are some people who see any slowing of their professional advancement, or even a less complimentary work evaluation, as "racially motivated." Other people may have a perceptual dark outlook on life.

This illustrates what the writer has named the "sunglasses attitude." If a person puts on sunglasses indoors, the dark lenses will make the room appear to be darker than it really is to all others in the room who are not wearing sunglasses. If a light meter were used in the room, one reading would be obtained if held in the hand, but a different reading would be obtained if the sunglasses were placed over the meter.

The point that is being made is that the amount of room light appears to all those who do not wear sunglasses to be at one level but appears to be darker to anyone who wears sunglasses. Because one person wears sunglasses and says that the room is darker does not make it the reality for others! The person who puts on sunglasses creates the very condition that he describes. If the person removes the sunglasses, then he would see the same amount of light in the room as the others.

The sunglasses attitude is an attitude that is assumed by an individual which darkens every view that he takes of the environment. Most do not wear sunglasses all the time but may put them on whenever faced with certain similar situations, such as work evaluations, teenagers, political parties, certain religions, races, and athletic events. The person creates the darkened conditions. He can change the condition if he wants, and if he is made aware of his limiting attitude that handicaps a clear perception of the situation. There has to be an awareness of the sunglasses attitude maintained by the individual and then a willingness on his part to change.

After awareness, the person has to believe that he is limiting his vision of a situation as it really exists to others. After the first stage of awareness and the second stage of acceptance of the belief that such an attitude exists, the person still has two more stages to work through to complete the change.

The third stage is to begin work to change the habit of donning the sunglasses. This takes a conscious effort to have a perception that the sunglasses must be removed at the forefront of all options. The fourth and final stage is to establish a constant practice so that the removal of the sunglasses attitude is complete, and the new habit of "seeing clearly" is established.

The sunglasses attitude is maintained by too many people in today's society. The attitude can be changed and must be changed if a person is to move beyond self-serving actions. The irony is that a person who wears the sunglasses attitude is almost always wrong, and while this is apparent to everyone else, the sunglasses wearer remains "blind."

Why do we wait until tomorrow to do what needs to be done today?

LIVING TODAY

There are a number of people who do not live "this day." Some of these people live in yesterday, even though they cannot change the things that happened yesterday. Many live on yesterday's memories of what was and ignore the present today. These people live for what was.

Many who live in yesterday are those whose happiest days were their high school or college days. Some of the high school or college athletes and cheerleaders who live their experiences over and over are good examples. Some are never quite able to make a success of today, and as time passes, their youthful experiences become more precious as their bodies age and thicken.

Others live only for the tomorrow's promised future. Today is ignored as they live for what might be and ignore today's "what is." Tomorrow, they are going to do... Oftentimes, they wear the "necklace of neglect." Their children are neglected, their homes, their relationships with others, and their assistance towards others are neglected.

Tomorrow," these people say, "I'm going to do this or that." And when tomorrow becomes today, the phrase is repeated again. Tomorrow becomes another forgotten today. As the months and years pass by, the number of tomorrows become more limited, yet these people still live for what they will become, or do, tomorrow.

I am not saying that we should not have goals for tomorrow. It is critical that we have something to which we can aim and which gives our lives a sense of direction. Albert Einstein in *Out of My Later Years* said, "Perfection of means and confusion of goals seem—in my opinion—to characterize our age." But the goals of tomorrow must come to fruition at some scheduled "today."

We cannot only be concerned with continual "becoming" something tomorrow. We must also be concerned with "being" today. Those about us whom we love deserve to have our best today. There is security in reliving the past, there is promise in living for tomorrow, but there is commitment in living today for others. We can control our todays for, essentially, that is all that we know we will have.

James Baldwin said, "No mortal lives that does not have regrets." When more time stretches behind than stretches before a person, some assessments, however reluctantly and incompletely, need to begin to be made. Between what one wishes to become and what one has become, there is a momentous gap. For those who live in the past and for those who live for the future, the gap increases. Only those who live today can truly enjoy tomorrow.

Why do we wait until tomorrow to do what needs to be done today?

LOCUS OF CONTROL

Many of us seem to constantly ask or comment as to who is in control of our lives. As children, we said that someone else made us do it or someone else made us angry. Too often, as adults, we continue that immature pattern. The immature pattern is one in which a person wants to assume responsibility when an action is a correct one but wants to put the blame elsewhere if the action is wrong.

There are two major locus-of-control views or concepts according to some psychologists: external and internal. The external-locus-of-control person believes that external factors control his destiny. The internal-locus-of-control person believes that he himself controls his own destiny. As a person perceives his locus of control, his future actions are then dictated by his personal view of the locus of control. In considering this, it is important to remember the *gestalt theory of psychology* which has a central contention that individuals see the world not as *it is,* but rather we see the world as *we are*!

The external-locus-of-control person believes that only external factors control his life and subsequent failure or success. He says things like "the government caused," "*they* made me," "the uptown bosses control," "society demands," "*they* don't like me because I am a minority or of the wrong religion, or not of their culture or value system," "the management holds me down," "the union will take care of me or the military brass will," or "the police are against me." In general, every failure is attributed to some external factor. The conversation is sprinkled with vague "theys" such as "they won't let me…" or "they said I had to…" As was once said, "A man who finds no satisfaction in himself seeks for it in vain elsewhere." If he loses a job, he was not the cause. If he enjoys success, it was given to him.

The internal-locus-of-control person believes that he himself is responsible for his ultimate success or failure. If he loses the job, he was the cause. If he obtains a high mark, it was because of his actions, not of others whom he knew. A typical attitude is that hard and sustained work will ultimately bring about rewards.

The internal-locus-of-control person accepts the concept that he or she is overweight because of his or her own eating habits. The external–locus-of-control person says, "I eat because," or "the whole family is overweight," or "I didn't gain weight until so-and-so did this to me," and so on. The internal person says, "I made a mistake," while the external looks for a reason, or another person, on which to fix the blame.

Motivation to change is lacking in the external-locus-of-control person. However, continual self-improvement is a key concept for most of the internal-locus-of-control individuals. This is one reason for the differences in success between the two types of focus-of-control persons.

In primitive societies, fate, or the gods, were believed to control their destinies. Rituals were established to try to win favor from those who controlled their lives. Many of the modern-day youth gangs are held together by a fear of the "external controllers" such as police, society, merchants, teachers, or others in positions of authority. This external focus is maintained by a number of adults who function in society. Such an external focus is highly susceptible to drug use, TV addiction, and other forms of escapism or daydreaming.

As Dr. Hugh Russell, a noted psychologist, said, "Believing we can do something does not necessarily allow us to do it. Yet it is very likely that if we believe that we cannot do something, this belief will tend to keep us from achieving it." The external-locus-of-control person lacks a belief in himself and in any future ability to improve himself or his situation.

The internal–locus-of-control person believes that he will go as far as his convictions and abilities will allow. In an increasingly dependent society, the welfare of the external-locus-of-control individuals will increasingly make demands on the internal-locus-of-control individual's achievements and work ethics. We need more internal-locus-of-control individuals who can accept and believe that they themselves make themselves successful as workers, as parents, as marriage partners, and as citizens. A belief system that "someone will take care of me no matter what I do or don't do," is the core of the external-locus-of-control person's process of living. Doing nothing and getting something is addictive.

A generation of believing in welfare will increase the number of participants who maintain the external locus of control. Because our society is a caring society, we reinforce the external-locus-of-control beliefs. The consequences of no action or insufficient action are not felt by most external-locus-of-control individuals. Yet there are many who escape the early childhood trap of following family traditions and whose accomplishments are not noticed. The acceptance of being responsible for one's own failures and/or successes is not a rewarded value in many instances.

Why do we wait until tomorrow to do what needs to be done today?

THE CHAINS OF HABIT

Some years ago, a story was told of an elephant in the St. Louis zoo that reached his trunk out over the zoo's moat, grasping the arm of a young girl handing him a peanut. Pulling the young girl over the moat and dropping her on the ground, the elephant got the peanut. The elephant's actions killed the girl.

The zoo officials decided not to kill the elephant as he had not previously displayed any hostile behavior. However, they placed a large stake in the middle of the compound and put a heavy chain with a metal band placed around the leg of the elephant that limited the distance the elephant could move. He could not come close to the moat to reach a visitor with his trunk.

A number of years passed and there were no indications of bad behavior from the elephant. The zoo officials removed the chain. But the zoo officials did not predict what would happen. The elephant did not move forward beyond the previous chain limited range of movement, even to pick up peanuts only inches from his trunk. The elephant was restrained in his forward movement by something stronger than a chain—the force of habit.

How many of us limit our behaviors because of the "chains of habit" that we have placed upon ourselves? The chains of habit may be good for us, such as the automatic street check before walking across the street. We may buckle our seatbelts, or we always brush our teeth.

However, what about our bad habits? Do we gossip about our friends, or are we sarcastic with our fellow workers, or are we so sure of our opinions that we allow no differing ones? Do we use too much salt, drink too many soft drinks? Are we always late for appointments? Do we always complain about the food in restaurants, and do we always leave our clothes on the floor?

Most of us cannot remember which shoe we put on first each morning. There is a need for these kinds of habits. Habits allow us to be more efficient. It has been conservatively estimated that some sixty to seventy percent of our behaviors are done under a "conditioning habit."

Most learned habits can be unlearned. If a bad habit is to be changed, only the person exhibiting the behavior can change it. There are five stages in the change: (1) awareness, (2) a strong desire to change, (3) sufficient and sustained motivation to change, (4) practice of the new habit desire and an extinguishing of the old habit, and (5) reinforcement of the newly acquired habit that is replacing the old habit.

We can replace bad habits with good habits. We can unchain ourselves from the bad habits and establish a positive and good habit. We need to tackle one bad habit at a time, and choosing an easy one to correct will give us confidence to tackle a more difficult bad habit. We may have to undo, avoid, replace, etc., a bad habit at least twenty-seven to thirty-seven times before it is extinguished. Some bad habits, such as smoking, require a multidisciplined approach and focused assistance.

Why do we wait until tomorrow to do what needs to be done today?

LISTENING INSTEAD OF HEARING

Many of us believe that we are good listeners when in fact we only hear well. We are like the Broadway producer who became convinced that he was losing his hearing. He went to the country's most famous ear specialist. After seating the producer in the chair, the specialist held a large pocket watch next to the producer's ear and asked if he could hear it. The producer could. The specialist walked about ten paces away and asked again if the producer could hear it. Impatiently, the producer said he could hear the watch ticking. The specialist then gave his diagnosis. He told the producer that there was nothing wrong with his hearing. The trouble was "that he wasn't listening."

A lot of misunderstanding and hurt feelings result from individuals failing to listen. People "hear" the words spoken by a spouse, a fellow worker, a child, or a friend. The literal meaning of the words are accepted at best. Sometimes if a person's attention is directed at something else, he only picks up the main words and he thinks he has received the main idea.

What is missed many times is the hidden message among or behind the spoken words. A person may say words that indicate something is not important, but a careful listening to the tone of the voice reveals that it is important. There is also the hidden-agenda message in some of the communications that is missed by the listener if the words are taken literally. As one mother told her child, "Don't do as I say, do as I want you to do."

Most people do not listen well when their attention is inner-directed. If someone is worrying about a problem at work, if a person is having a personal problem with someone about whom he cares, or if a person is in a "mental-coasting phase," then very little listening can be expected. Many make the mistake of saying something twice, thinking surely the other will listen the second time around. Others try volume to ensure listening. Both methods fail.

If the goal is to want the other person(s) to listen, then a person must pick the right time, place, and situation. A person must look into the other's eyes to obtain full attention and avoid the cliché of "you never listen to me" as a preface to attempt to ensure listening this time. People must say what they mean and be open, direct, and honest. Ensuring that others are listening is also a responsibility for public speakers because of the size and variety of listeners with whom the speaker is trying to communicate.

Two more suggestions for communicating by individuals are to keep the important messages concise and to speak in a measured voice while maintaining eye contact. The value of face-to-face communication is critical. Too many people use texting, e-mail, or cell phone calls to try to communicate thoughts and feelings that instead need face-to-face, voice-to-ear, eye-to-eye personal interactions. Individuals need to understand what is meant before they can do what is expected as a result of the communication. Some individuals may not want to do what has been communicated and therefore say either they did not hear, or did not understand, what was said.

Ironically, some people may hear the conversation better when loud music is prevalent. However, the best chance of good communication is face to face and eye to eye with very little space between the speaker and the listener. Cell phones need to be off, and the ears need to be clear. If people want to hear, usually they can. Avoid too much repetition and favorite points as boredom kills attention. Finally, a person should not beat around the bush or beat it to death.

Why do we wait until tomorrow to do what needs to be done today?

EXAMINING CRITICISM

A positive way of regarding criticism is to think of it as a measure of being successful. To modify Mark Twain's comment, "Let us be thankful for critics. But for them, the rest of us could not know our level of success." It might be surprising to learn that sometimes criticism is a secret yearning to be similar to the person being criticized or wanting someone to be better than the person offering the criticism. The Little League parent who yells criticism of the young child probably didn't do any better at the game when the parent participated as a child, if the parent had participated.

One has to look at criticism with an objective view. Usually only about one-third of criticism is reasonably accurate. The other two-thirds are usually from people who are envious, jealous, unhappy of themselves and thus want to make someone else feel the same way. Some people have the same faults, and thus by telling someone else to correct the faults that they themselves cannot correct, they find a type of tension reduction. An example would be a fat person telling another that he or she should go on a diet.

The first step for a person is to determine if there is some truth in the criticism aimed at his behaviors. If there is, how much of the criticism that is true is within a person's capacity to correct? Used in the right manner, criticism may provide the impetus to begin improvement of one's self. This objective review of the criticism is necessary. Blindly closing one's eyes to justified criticism is like walking blindfolded across a busy street.

But if one determines that the criticism is unjustified, one has basically two choices: to ignore it or to react to it. Ninety-seven percent of the time, a person should ignore the unjustified criticism. The other three percent may require some response from a person, but only after consideration of the consequences of any verbal response or action taken. Any type of response to criticism is high-risk behavior with possible physical or verbal retaliation.

However, sometimes if there is no response, it may be believed by others as an *admitted guilt* to the criticism that had been directed at the individual. Below are some responses that can be used by one in a private conversation with oneself. Seldom, if ever, should one use these responses publicly.

Some favorites are:

Few slanders can stand the wear of silence.

Often the surest way to convey misinformation
is to tell the truth.

> Some critics and babies are alike. Both have a
> lot of noise on one end and a complete lack
> of responsibility on the other.

> Criticism is rarely inhibited by ignorance.

Individuals need to be careful in using the above responses. More problems may develop than what can be anticipated. Exhibiting good manners is the proper behavior to exhibit in responding to unjustified criticism. As Dr. William J. Reilly said, "Our main problem is how to get along with people in spite of their imperfections and in spite of our own."

Why do we wait until tomorrow to do what needs to be done today?

REFRIGERATOR EMOTIONS

Refrigerator emotions are those emotions that have been kept in check or, in the slang terminology, "kept cool." A cold emotion is not capable of giving, and thus receiving in return, the warmth needed as man interacts with man. The ability of man to feel emotions is one of the two differences that separate man from other animals. Yet there is a tendency among many men and women to keep their emotions in check—to put their feelings into the refrigerator, so to speak.

Most people understand that unvented anger may erupt unexpectedly. Other emotions such as jealousy or envy also can have a heated eruption. But perhaps, the most needed emotion that man possesses, the emotion of love, is put too often into the refrigerator. Love is put away so as not to spoil, and thus, the daily nutrition and balance to life that love provides is not available to the individual.

People tend to put love in the refrigerator for a variety of reasons. An unhappy love affair, divorce, the death of a loved one, or a time-consuming career are a few of the reasons that love is put on the refrigerator shelf. Just as our body needs certain vitamins and minerals to maintain physical health, our minds need the nutrition of warm and healthy emotions. We need emotional meals to fulfill our mental needs just like we need nutritional food to satisfy our physical hunger.

Just as the feast-and-famine program of eating is not beneficial to our physical bodies, our mental needs can best be met with a continuous supply of needed emotions. Love must be one emotion obtained on a daily or weekly basis. Just as crowded movies, ball games, and shopping malls fulfill the basic need of "skin hunger," or the need to be touched by other people, we need to have the emotional interaction with others to sustain our emotional health.

There are two extremes to avoid. There are those who gorge on their emotions and become too satiated to really feel, and then there are those who have refrigerated their emotions, maybe even freezing their emotions. Some may feel that they are saving their emotions for a "leftover meal." However, leftover emotional meals provide the participant a hungry and unsatisfied life.

What we put in, we can take out. What we give to others will return to us. Feeding the emotional need a full meal of love is the best way of not having "spoiled leftovers" when one needs a meal. True emotions sometimes appear to be extremes of opposites. There is the intense fire of hate or the freezing out of a relationship. There is the heat of jealousy and the coldness of rejection. There is the warmth of love and the comfort of friendship. The realization and the acceptance of the range of human emotions is a mark of maturity.

Why do we wait until tomorrow to do what needs to be done today?

SMOTHER LOVE

One of the oldest movie clichés is the line, "Because I love you so much, I must let you go." Yet many of us still do not see this simplistic statement being inherent with wisdom. As parents in particular, we want to hang on to our children for as long as we can.

Social scientists have said that modern Americans create an enforced adolescence until the children are through college. We as parents are trying so hard to make sure that our children do not have to go through the rough times that we had to go through, that we unrealistically solve life's problems for our children. We continually maintain this ease of living for our children. At its worst, this process makes our children emotional hostages and at its best, we can claim we love them too much to let them go.

We are afraid to allow our children to "stub their toes." What we forget is that because of the stubbed toes that we received while we were growing up, we are what we are, i.e., our past failures helped us to be the success that we are today. A prime example is of the father who worked long, hard hours during his high school years, put himself through college, and became a successful businessman. This father then says, "My child is not going to have to work his way through school."

The problem of "smother love" may increase in future years. A demographic study done in 1989 predicted that only forty-five percent of the high school graduates of the year 2000 would have the traditionally intact family. Some forty percent would have parents who divorce before the graduate is eighteen years old, and five percent will have parents who separate. Some twelve percent will be born to an unwed mother, and two percent will have a parent die before graduation. While current statistics for the past two years are varied because of other factors (immigration, increased mobility, new definitions of households) being studied, most educators and social workers agree that those earlier numbers were accurate. A new element is the single parent marrying again in greater numbers.

Because of the loss of a spouse, for whatever reason, the remaining spouse (many times the mother) may tend to hang on to the child for the parent's own emotional support. A type of you-must-love-me-and-not-let-me-down atmosphere surrounds such a child. The beginning of resentment for the role the child must adopt is fueled by the smother love of the parent.

It was Oscar Wilde who, in *A Woman of No Importance,* said, "Children begin by loving their parents. After a time, they judge them. Rarely, if ever, do they forgive them." A child who is a recipient of smother love will only rarely forgive. Distance in space, time, and emotions are the usual tactics that eventually force the separation and the death of smother love. It is ironic that what we as parents want most is lost because of too much love. Growth and independence is inevitable; and for a parent to try to contain either is to stunt the child, lose the child, or create an unacceptable response or social misfit.

Why do we wait until tomorrow to do what needs to be done today?

HAPPINESS IS SHARING

In the 1962 movie, *Days of Wine and Roses*, Jack Lemmon and Lee Remick tear through a greenhouse looking for a hidden bottle of whiskey. They received Oscar and Golden Globe nominations for their wrenching performances as a young couple torn by alcoholism. In the film, frustrated by their lack of alcohol, they begin tearing the plants apart looking for the bottle. Symbolically, however, when Jack Lemmon finds the bottle, he hides the bottle from Lee Remick. In the movie, he was selfish.

Yet while we feel critical toward Jack Lemmon's selfish actions, we are just as guilty in many ways of our own day-to-day behaviors. Too many times we are selfish with our time, our praise, and our actions to assist others who may be needing us. We need to share ourselves with others who need us or who need a portion of our time.

We dash through the greenhouse of life, looking for some item or items to bring us happiness. Sometimes, we share that search with a spouse or with family members. The problem is that we get so caught up in the search for happiness that we forget to share ourselves with others, and thereby, many times we deny others that which we are seeking ourselves.

The mother who does not have time to tell a child a story, or the father who does not attend the child's baseball game are some examples. The older brother who will not drive his sister to a birthday party, the sister who will not help her brother with his homework, and the neighbor who does not take time to visit a sick friend in the hospital are other examples.

Happiness is not something that can be enjoyed alone. Sharing our time, our praise, and our actions to help others is the first step toward obtaining happiness. Sometimes we think that we have found the bottle of happiness, but like the actor in the movie, we do not want to share it with anyone else. Perhaps we are afraid, as Jack Lemmon was in the film, that once it is shared, the liquid of happiness would soon be gone.

On the contrary, happiness shared has the unexplainable result of increasing. While such results cannot be explained by scientific laws, the spiritual happiness obtained is apparent for those who have shared and who have become recipients of increasing amounts of happiness.

Giving happiness is obtaining it. Obtaining happiness is sharing it, and by sharing it, one's own happiness is increased. Too few people will believe this. These people will continue their frantic search for happiness through the greenhouse of life. When and if they find it, and selfishly consume it, they will lose it.

Why do we wait until tomorrow to do what needs to be done today?

THE PROCESSIONARY CATERPILLAR

There are many people who do the routine tasks and remain in the background. "Old what's-his-name," or "you know, the wallflower," or the "quiet, mousy wife," are all terms that indicate that someone is a background person who lives a life of sameness. These people may do the same things day in and day out, with a kind of desperate fervor, similar to the processionary caterpillar.

Jean Fabre, a French naturalist, discovered a unique caterpillar in South America. The caterpillar seemed to follow blindly any other caterpillar in front. Entire lines of caterpillars would be strung out along the various branches. As they moved along a branch, they would be nose to tail.

Fabre tried an experiment. He took a line of the processionary caterpillars and placed them on the top of a large flower pot that contained a leafy flower. He took the lead caterpillar of the chain and placed him behind the last caterpillar in the line.

The caterpillars began to march around the top edge of the flower pot. For days they marched until they dropped from hunger and exhaustion. Only inches away was food in the form of the leafy flower, but the "following the caterpillar ahead" was so imprinted that none could break the circling chain.

There are many people who tramp about an endless circle, living quiet lives of monotony and dullness. These people follow someone else's lead constantly. Day in and day out the same routines are followed, or else there is too little a change made so that one could see any different behavior.

Instead of staring straight ahead, these people should look about and see a variety of their choices. Renewal of tired spirits, fresh challenges, and many useful accomplishments would be theirs if they would only break out of the processionary cycle. It is ironic that the more desperate they become, the greater the habitual routine of the processionary cycle is followed.

The familiarity of sameness breeds comfort and security. For some the price is not too high. The dullness of knowing what to expect and to do is less frightening than to try out the unfamiliar or to do something different. The unknown is frightening to the insecure or to the person who suffered a significant failure.

The processionary person is a most unhappy individual. Unlike the caterpillar, we have feelings and a mind that craves expression and creativity. The processionary person leads a life of quiet desperation, dreading the arrival of another dull tomorrow. Routines must be followed and only the change of the seasons and the possibility of celebrating holidays result in a change. The tragedy is that the person may not be aware of the availability of a more fulfilling life.

Why do we wait until tomorrow to do what needs to be done today?

GROUP THINKING

There is a tendency for many people to avoid having to make a personal decision when the consequences of their decision may greatly affect their lives. Instead of saying, "I have decided to…," there are many people who preface their decision by saying, "Most people…," or "Others have…," or similar personal decision disclaimers.

The individuals who avoid taking responsibility for making their own decisions become trapped by a "group think" decision-making style. Instead of saying "I think…," these people say, "The group thinks…," and thus the worry of making a wrong decision is lessened, because after all, the collective wisdom of the group should supersede the individual wisdom of one.

There is even a subgroup of group thinkers who can be recognized by comments like, "What do you think of…?" or "What do most people feel…?" or other introductory phrases. These individuals usually have several key people whom they sound out for advice before making a decision. Instead of "What does the group think?" it is limited to a "What does *my* group think?" orientation.

Still, the same basic weakness underlies each method. Instead of thinking as individuals and making decisions, there are those people who utilize the concept of group thinking and make decisions by what they believe the group would decide. There are many times that a group decision may be the best decision. There may be times when individuals need to use the group-think method of reaching a decision. The problem develops when the group-think decision method is constantly utilized.

Americans have long prided themselves that the majority of the people should govern the needs of all by protecting the rights of the minorities. Thus, the decision reached by many has been instilled in most as a basic way to determine the truth. Americans place great faith in all sorts of polls, predictions of stock market analyses, fashion designers, song charts, etc. There are many "expert" individuals and groups who claim expertise and are only too willing to tell people what to think.

Finally, the people who have trouble making personal decisions dislike the feeling of uncertainty. This feeling makes them easily trapped by many group-think organizations who emphatically state such and such is so. The group-think organizations are not uncertain about their beliefs. Of course, the realization that another group-think organization has an opposite belief is conveniently ignored. During political elections, the group-think person desperately clings to his own group's thinking and beliefs.

There are many organizations who would think for everyone. There are many organizations who demand blind loyalty and allegiance to their beliefs and practices, and thus would provide all with the group-think method for decision making. Some religious cults fill this need for group thinking.

But individuals need to think for themselves, decide for themselves, and be responsible for themselves. After all, individuals live with the decisions after they are made. There is a feeling of accomplishment and a feeling of self-worth obtained by making informed decisions by oneself or in cooperation with a significant other, such as a spouse. Decisions that impact another may require a sharing of the decision-making process. Money expenditures is one such example. More individuals need to think for themselves and not get caught up by societal fads or fan worship or a TV cult following, or university "frat" thinking, or advertising-victim addiction. Monitor or ignore the thinking from the golf group or office club, or the snares of successful athletic teams, or other lures of temporarily feeling successful by attaching oneself to those who are.

Why do we wait until tomorrow to do what needs to be done today?

THE LADY'S PROFILE

Research has shown us that we see what we want to see. The 1964 book *Human Behavior: An Inventory of Scientific Findings* by Bernard Berelson and Gary Steiner listed some 1,045 findings. One finding was that people see what they "need" to see. "The pupil of the eye dilates on seeing pleasant things and contracts at distasteful things. The more ambiguous the view, the more it arouses preconceptions." It was reported that seeing is so subjective that coins of the same size looked bigger to poor children than to rich children.

Look at the Lady's Profile on the next page. What is seen? How old is the lady? Is she under thirty or over fifty? Is she attractive or an old hag?

Illustration 2

Some people may have seen that the profile contains the profiles of *two* women: One is of an old lady with a deeply sunk chin. The other is of a young lady, looking three-quarters to the left. The nose of the old lady becomes the chin of the young lady, and the mouth of the old lady becomes a necklace on the young. The young lady's nose is barely seen at the left.

Sometimes when we see something, we develop a mental set that makes it difficult for us to see something different. Two people can look at this profile and each can see a different lady. Imagine the argument that each puts to the other, and both are wrong if they say that only one lady is shown. If only one image is seen, the person is only half right.

We can look at the same thing, see the same object and still perceive it differently from the others. We disagree with someone's decision because we see the situation differently. It is no wonder that we disagree with a referee's call or another's political view.

Awareness of real differences in views and accepting the belief that others might be just as correct is the beginnings of true wisdom. A religious person does not have to accept the belief of an atheist but can acknowledge that that person does believe differently. Effective interacting with others and communicating in a clear manner could be improved by remembering the above illustration. We can be more accurate, more understanding of others, and more careful of our opinions. We can and should maintain a core of inner beliefs that will not be lost by tolerance.

Why do we wait until tomorrow to do what needs to be done today?

PROCRUSTEAN BELIEFS

There are some people who live limited lives because of their limited beliefs. Some hold on to a small personal belief even when faced with large amounts of reality. These people maintain what is sometimes called a "procrustean belief." It is a belief held contrary to fact or what most people hold to be truthful or accept as being truthful.

In Greek mythology, Procrustes was an innkeeper who boasted that he had a bed that would fit any guest. In those days, the travelers were men, and even then, the heights of the men varied, ranging from dwarfs to tall individuals. Those ancient travelers stayed overnight in inns.

Procrustes would wager with various guests, sometimes after long hours of drinking, that he had a bed that would fit any guest, no matter how short or how tall. Most of the guests selected for the wager would bet because Procrustes would choose short or tall men. He said all would fit in his famous bed. Many tall and short guests accepted the bet.

Procrustes, according to the story, always won. He won because he made the guest "fit the bed." Procrustes would convince the guest to allow him to tie the guest's hands to the iron front of the bed, so that Procrustes "could measure more accurately." Procrustes would tie the man's arms securely to the headboard. If the guest was too short for the bed, Procrustes would use a small winch with which he would pull a rope that he had tied around the ankles. He would pull on the winch until the man's length fit the bed. With the short man's arms tied to the headboard, the pulley action caused the legs to be pulled from the torso. By doing this, the man was made to "fit the bed." Procrustes always got the money for the wager first.

If the man was too long for the bed, Procrustes would cut off the man's legs. Again, he would tie the guest's arms to the iron headboard, "for measurement purposes," and then allow the guest to extend his legs over the end of the bed. He would use an ax to ensure that the legs were cut off to fit inside the bottom of the footboard.

Procrustes made each man fit the bed, rather than have the bed adjusted to the man. There are some people who adjust their beliefs in the same way. The people with procrustean beliefs make the facts fit their preconceived belief. Evidence that is contrary to their belief is ignored or made a source of amusement.

A good example of this belief is that held by people who belong to the Flat Earth Society. This society still believes that the earth is flat. The TV pictures taken from space is trick photography, they say. They live their lives believing that the earth is flat.

Beliefs are not always negative. Beliefs are needed and justified. For instance, religious faith is a justified belief. A number of inventions and discoveries developed because someone ignored or did not believe the facts that others accepted. A person must believe in himself even when others may not. There are needed convictions that evolve from beliefs as well as values, traditions, and loyalties.

Perhaps we could examine some of our beliefs objectively with obtained factual information. Are we making the facts fit the belief? Are we cutting short the deductions or drawing out the wrong conclusions? Just because we cherish a long-held belief, is it the appropriate one for us? Or, more importantly, is it correct?

Why do we wait until tomorrow to do what needs to be done today?

MONDAY-MORNING QUARTERBACK

The Monday-morning quarterback was a phrase developed in the sports world to describe the self-styled, amateur football coaches who, after the football game was over, were heard to say, "I wouldn't have called that play," or, "If I were the coach, I would have called a pass play instead of a run." After the game is over, the Monday-morning quarterbacks always had a critique of how the coach called the plays during the heat and pressure of the game.

Even sports writers, who should know better, oftentimes would get caught in second-guessing the plays called by the coach. The term drifted over into basketball, baseball, and other sports. However, the tendency to second-guessing another's decision or action is not restricted to the sports world. Monday-morning quarterbacking is prevalent among the business world and among friends and relatives.

The Monday-morning quarterback (MMQ) syndrome is prevalent in all walks of life. Many may have this syndrome and may not be aware of it. When one hears the phrase, "If it had been my child…" or, "If it had been me, I would have…" Even one's friends or coworkers may make similar comments. Even ministers' sermons are subjected to criticism.

How many of us second-guess the decisions that our friends or our employers have had to make? Many times we are right with our second-guess because of the advantage of having time or hindsight, or, after the decision was made, additional information became available to us that was not available to the original decision maker. It is also easier to make a decision when one does not have to live with the consequences or when emotions are not involved.

Why do we wait until the decision is made to offer our advice as to what to decide? One needs to avoid the MMQ or professional Monday-morning quarterback. The professional MMQ is so busy redoing other people's decisions that oftentimes his own life is a mess. Many times, that most indecisive person on decisions that impacts him personally can be the most decisive MMQ regarding another's decisions.

The MMQ is an individual who is aloof from the game, making judgments about an earlier decision in the game. What we need is an on-the-spot assistant coach who volunteers to the head coach information to assist the man living with the decision before the decision is made. We can help our friends if help is needed or desired with this type of approach. Free advice is worth exactly what it costs—nothing. Some of our friends or relatives or fellow employees do not desire our advice and certainly do not appreciate an MMQ's opinion.

We are all capable of making wrong decisions. As Alexander Pope said, "Whoever thinks a faultless piece to see, thinks what ne'er was not is nor e'er shall be." We do not need others to point out our wrong decisions so much as we need assistance and advice before the decision is made. Instead of being a Monday-morning quarterback, become a friendly advisor. Again, it is critical to keep in mind that all people will make a bad decision. There is no need to relate the obvious bad decision to a person who is already berating himself for it.

Why do we wait until tomorrow to do what needs to be done today?

SOLVING LIFE'S PREDICAMENTS

A number of writers and philosophers have tried to describe the process of life. Santayana had written a practical description: "Life is not a spectacle or a feast: it is predicament." Life then is not merely a movie to be viewed as happening to others nor is it a surface involvement to enjoy only the pleasures of life. Life, it would appear, is a series of predicaments that must be successfully resolved.

The problem then becomes *How does one resolve the predicaments?* or *How does one solve life's problems?* The first step for most individuals is to master a decision-making strategy. If a problem or predicament faces an individual, the choices or alternatives may range from two to hundreds. There is an inherent pleasure in successfully solving a difficult life problem.

The following decision-making strategy will provide one method to analyze the choices or alternatives in order to make a decision to resolve the predicament. There are five steps. This strategy works best when the steps are written out.

Step one: A person should think and then write out what he *should do*. Most of the time there are laws, rules, social dictates, or a conscience directive as to what one should do. Either the individual or others feel that a particular action should be done.

Step two: The person writes down what he *wants to do*. Sometimes an individual knows what he should do, but finds himself wanting to do something else. There may be several things that he wants to do, but all should be written down.

Step three: Next, the person should write out all the *alternatives* for the things that he had decided that he should do and then write out the alternatives for the things that he wants to do.

Step four: Now the person writes out the *consequence(s)* for each of the listed alternatives. It could be a good consequence (someone is made happy by that choice), or it could be a bad consequence (possible arrest and imprisonment could result).

Step five: The final stage is the *actual decision-making process*. The individual should study the alternatives and consequences. The final step is what he *will do*, after weighing the alternatives and the consequences of each. If time allows, "sleeping over the decision" is helpful.

In summary, this decision-making strategy involves five steps. An individual has to think of: (1) what he *should do*, (2) what he *wants to do*, (3) *alternatives* for doing what he should do and also for what he wants to do, (4) *consequences* of each of the actions considered, and (5) what he finally *will do* after the consideration of the other four steps.

An individual cannot resolve all of life's predicaments by using this five-step method. However, continued practice will indicate to most individuals that it is a simple and practical strategy that will work many times. It should be remembered that this is for an individual's own decision-making process. When the decision involves another person's interests or needs, or other life-sustaining or life-fulfilling consequences, then this method must be modified. For example, a decision to have a baby involves both parents. This decision-making model can be adapted to two people if both are involved in working together through the various stages.

Why do we wait until tomorrow to do what needs to be done today?

GULLIVER'S STRINGS

In today's busy world, we begin finding ourselves seemingly trapped with too many things tying us down. We feel like that we have no place to go, nothing to do when we get there, and that there is nothing that we can do to change the feeling of being tied to a job, the home, or some situation. We find ourselves unable to move or to change or break away.

In the book *Gulliver's Travels*, Gulliver comes to the land of the little people. He falls asleep, and when he wakes up, he cannot move as he finds himself tied down with many, many small strings. He is tied down, not with a few large cables or ropes, but rather is held helpless by many small strings. Likewise, we allow ourselves to become helpless by being tied with too many small strings.

There is tendency for us to look for some large items holding us down. We begin to blame the spouse, the boss, the job, the economic conditions, the political scene, the unions, the OPEC nations and so on for the trapped feeling that we have. We would rather it be some big item that we can see as tangible and outside of our control. In that way, we can affix blame on someone or something besides ourselves and thus not have to take responsibility to change the situation.

The concept that we are causing our own problems, that we are trapping ourselves, and that the trapping items are small ones that we can change, can be unsettling. There is always quick denial. We are heard to say such things as, "I'm not responsible for..." or "They won't let me..." When we look for the obvious and big things tying us down, we make a basic mistake of ignoring the many small things that gain strength by quantity. A brick wall gains its strength by the quantity of its bricks. To tear down a brick wall, we begin with a brick at a time.

Likewise, when we feel trapped, we should look for the many small items that are tying us down or trapping us. We begin by untying the easiest strings, and with the confidence of success, we can begin to tackle the larger ones. With our directed and concentrated attention given to the many small strings that are holding us back, we can begin the process of breaking away. We begin with one small string at a time.

Why do we wait until tomorrow to do what needs to be done today?

BIGGER AND FASTER

This is a tendency to believe that anything new is better, and that if something is different, faster, bigger, etc., then it must be better. The words "new and improved" will sell the same product at a higher price for many shoppers. We are creatures of habit when shopping. Most psychologists tell us that ingrained shopping habits are what sell most products. We fall victim to advertising fads because of the hidden messages that are projected along with the apparent advertising.

For example, soft drink commercials would have us believe that all we have to do to achieve instant popularity is to drink their product. The question is do we buy the product because it has a distinctive taste and we like it? Or do we buy it because unconsciously we think buying it will help us to become someone that we are not? After several times of asking for a particular product, the "buying habit" takes over and another advertising addict is added to the Madison Avenue advertising success story.

If any product guarantees us that it is "the fastest," "the biggest," "the best," or "the newest," we fall into the consumer trap of "keeping up with the times." Of course, if we cannot make a decision between conflicting claims as to which product is the best, the advertisers help us by saying, "More doctors use…" or by presenting some movie idol who endorses a particular shampoo or other product. It is assumed that the movie idol has carefully screened the other products, as this movie idol has a public responsibility. However, ninety-nine percent of the time, an endorsement is made because the price (for the movie idol) was right. It's just a shorter version of acting.

What is ironic is that some of the most successfully advertised products are not any better than any of the more generic brands; however, we pay more for the more highly advertised product. Somehow, we Americans believe that we "pay for quality" and thus, the more that it costs, the better it must be. Because different is not better, bigger is not better, and faster is not better, we need to stop becoming a repeat advertising victim and instead become a realistic and practical consumer. We will live longer and live better when we do.

Finally, many of us become a sale-saving victim. Too many times a purchase of a sale item is made not because of need, or even a desire for the product, but rather the sale is concluded because it was a bargain. "Below cost" or even "fifty percent off" this item, or the sneaky "buy one and get one free" sales promotions make usually rational thinkers victims of the savings pitch.

Why do we wait until tomorrow to do what needs to be done today?

THERE IS NO WISDOM PRESCRIPTION

In today's world, we have a tendency to look for "prescriptions" for our minds. We look for concrete answers in "capsule form" to diminish the pain of the inquiring mind. Witness the fix-it books on topics of stress, divorce, child-rearing, management, thinking and so on.

We assuage our inquiring mind with the "aspirins" of other people thoughts. It is rather like watching a movie instead of reading the novel. Our imagination must conjure up a novel's described picture of the characters, but in the movie the character is completely revealed to us. And how many times has the movie not measured up to the imaginative reading of the novel?

Our best teachers assist their students by introducing them to areas of knowledge. These teachers introduce and then allow each individual to grow at a speed and in a direction which sustains a pursuit of answers unimagined by the teacher. The teacher does not tell the student what he (teacher) knows but instead introduces the student to the beginning of knowledge.

The philosopher Martin perhaps said it best: "The most that a teacher can do for a student is to effect a few introductions. After that, it is a matter of his own capacity for devotion."

St. Thomas (*De Veritate*, XII, 6) said, "Our mind is not the mirror of eternity, but the mirror of time." It would seem then that it takes time to develop the mind to the point where wisdom begins its maturing process. Experiences are also a factor in assisting or hindering learning. Somewhere in the entire process, creativity is born.

It may not be possible for the young and the quick to be able to have wisdom but may merely become acquainted with the potential. Recent research from Bowling Green State University in Ohio indicated that reflective judgment begins in the teen years and goes through some stages to a higher level of reflective judgment. A number of people, thirty-five to fifty years of age still lack this ability to have the higher level of reflective judgment although most individuals in this age group do have the ability. However, a number of individuals have the ability to employ and to enjoy reflective judgment but do not.

One cannot know wisdom from the outside, but one can learn of it from others. Some people enjoy growing flowers while others enjoy the picked bouquet. While the teacher can plant the seeds of knowledge, the individual student must nurture the growth. The growth process of the mind takes time. There is no quick-release capsule or even a prescription for wisdom.

In brief, there are no prescriptions for our minds as we seek wisdom, only introductions. The mirror of time reflects the growth of knowledge and the development of wisdom. It would appear that we have many men and women who have knowledge but most of whom may not develop wisdom. Some philosophers believe that true wisdom only comes with age, some believe that wisdom comes from experiences, especially suffering experiences, and others believe that knowledge and time develop wisdom. It is possible that all are right.

Why do we wait until tomorrow to do what needs to be done today?

MAKING THE BLUES

Many of us get caught up in the belief that having "the blues" is fashionable, acceptable, and inevitable. We hear about the morning-after blues, the Monday morning blues, the holiday blues, the time-of-the-month blues, the budget blues, and many others. All of the various blues have one common denominator: the blues are felt to reflect a feeling of depression, of being down, with subsequent low levels of mental, emotional, or physical energies.

Having the blues appears acceptable to others as an excuse to act the way the condition implies. In other words, the expectation creates the condition. When one says, "I have the blues about…," the condition develops. The belief in blues gives rise to its development. Outside of medical documentation of physiological basis, blues are nothing more than a role-playing of a poor-little-me role or a pity-me role, or an I've-got-an-excuse-for-my-behavior role.

At best then, the blues serve only as an excuse to (1) not do anything, or (2) do something one wanted to do anyway but were afraid of the consequences. A sharp retort is excused by saying, "I've had the blues today," and a failure to complete the needed work is excused by saying, "I've had the blues today." Ironically, once the blues excuse is used, the condition develops and then worsens. The belief causes the condition.

Habit can be friend or foe. The blues belief and subsequent actions to carry out the blues expectations in thinking, feeling, and action behaviors can lead to the establishment of a habit that becomes a deadly, weakening foe. One can begin to anticipate, even welcome with a masochistic glee, the advent of the Monday-morning blues until every Monday morning becomes a dreadful day. The belief that Monday morning is going to be bad, backed by past Monday morning actions that made it so, sets the cycle for thoughts, feelings, and actions to develop that expectation.

Sure enough, with little surprise, the Monday-morning blues, or other blues, arrive on time and on target. If a person can cause the blues to develop, then he has the ability to make the blues dissolve. This means accepting responsibility for one's actions and mental frame of mind. There is no cloak of blame that can be used to hide an avoidance of responsibility for one's actions. The last few chapters give a method to overcome the blues habit of reference.

Why do we wait until tomorrow to do what needs to be done today?

DO WE HAVE TO HAVE CERTAINTY IN OUR LIVES?

Many people attempt to arrange their lives into predictable patterns based upon some seemingly scientific basis for success. The uncertainty of not knowing what will happen next makes many people's lives become anxious moments while awake and nightmares while asleep. This belief develops from this scientific age where we utilize scientific technology to diagnose and computers to predict events. It is easy to believe that the current scientific methods can help with human relationships.

Most people are unaware of the errors within even the scientific method. For over three hundred years, physicists debated the definition of light. The first group agreed that light transmittal was through waves. The second group of physicists believed that light was transmitted through a series of particles. Each group had the formulas and experiments that proved its theory was correct.

However, in 1900, physicist Max Planck presented a new theory that light was transmitted dually by both the wave and the particle process. Planck's hypothesis that light was released in distinct packets, or quanta of energy, challenged the known basis of physics. Modern experiments have confirmed the quantum theory that light behaves in a manner that supports both the wave and particle theories. Thus, light does indeed have a wave-particle duality.

Even though many people realize that science is still in the process of discovery and ever-changing theories as new information emerges, these same people want the exactness of predictions that the scientific world appears to offer. The need for security "blinds" these people to the essential human quality of adaptability that is unique to human race. Because of the individual differences and the variety of experiences that each person has, predictability is not available.

Some people have a need for certainty in their lives because of their fear of failure. These individuals do not want to fail, so all precautions are taken to ensure that success, or at least there are high odds that their action(s) would occur. The irony is that this fear of failure may cause failure because of this apprehension.

In 1976, George Wallenda fell from a tightrope while performing in San Juan, Puerto Rico. Afterwards, his wife was interviewed and she said that her husband had become "possessed" that he would fall. The thought that he would fall this time was thought to have caused his fall, as before he had successfully walked the tightrope many times. This fear of failure concept became known as the Wallenda factor.

To answer the question "Do we have to have certainty in our lives?" the answer is no. To have too much certainty begins the decaying process of the creative mind. Too much "certainty comfort" insulates a person from the realities of a changing world and kills the conquering spirit of the American pioneer. We need the certainty of belief in ourselves and in some others for a balance, but we do not need the amount of certainty that so many desperately seek. We do not have to have certainty in our lives.

Why do we wait until tomorrow to do what needs to be done today?

JANUS

Janus was the god of doors and gates in Roman mythology. January, the first month in the Julian calendar, is named after him. The ancient Romans prayed to Janus before beginning anything new. Because a person symbolically goes through a door (or in ancient times a gate into a walled city), Janus became associated with the beginning of things. He was usually pictured with two faces, one looking forward to the future, and one looking backward to the past.

In our own lives, we should periodically take the posture of Janus. By that is meant while in the present, we should look toward the future to determine what needs to be done or accomplished. It must be started now. But, like Janus, we must look back upon the past to give us some guidance from our past experiences, our past failures and successes, and our past unfulfilled dreams.

Many of us make New Year's resolutions faithfully each year. These resolutions usually have something to do with improving something(s) about ourselves. This is always done on New Year's Day, January 1. It would seem appropriate as we begin a new year that we would make some improvements in our lives, either for ourselves personally or for someone that we love.

The problem that exists is that most of us make these New Year's resolutions because (1) everyone else is doing it, (2) it is expected of us to complete a list, and (3) no one really blames us if we fail to carry out the resolution. An example of a favorite resolution on New Year's is to lose weight. This attempt usually lasts a few weeks, and then it's back to business as usual—a full meal and an expanding waistline.

We need to refocus our thinking into positive action. First of all, Janus is associated with January, but a true resolution to improve can begin at any time. If we look back into the past and find something to improve about ourselves, we must take action now to bring about the needed change in the future. In other words, our personal Janus can be now. What the Romans believed to be a yearly beginning, we can make of it a daily happening.

Some historians have said that Janus was pictured as standing with one foot in the past and one foot in the future. In our own lives, we stand much in the same manner. The bridge between the past and the future is our existing body that is currently involved with the present. The present is the bridge between the past (what was) and the future (what might be).

From this abstract presentation to a realistic implementation evolves the challenges that the courageous accept and the timid avoid. What separates the great men from the small men in history and in the present is *action*. When we act upon our future goals, we break away from the rank and file of ordinary people who wait for things to happen to them. When we act, we are making things happen.

What we need to do then is to continually have Janus moments in our daily lives. We need to stop and take stock of what we have done and what we have yet to do. While the Janus of Roman mythology symbolized a beginning, the Janus moments of our lives should be the initiators of new actions. This is a continuous process for self-improvement and progress that is real.

Why do we wait until tomorrow to do what needs to be done today?

TAKE A DEEP SEAT

The writer was reared on a ranch and his dad passed on his favorite bits of cowboy lore. One of the favorites was this saying, "Take a deep seat and a faraway look!" This message was told to the bronc rider who was preparing to ride an unbroken horse, sometimes known as a bronc. An outlaw bronc usually ended up on the rodeo circuit.

This saying has a literal meaning. When told to "take a deep seat," the bronc rider was reminded to dig into the saddle and curl his body to be ready to take the first plunge of the bucking bronc. He needed to tighten his legs about the barrel of the horse and in essence try to plaster the seat of his pants to the saddle.

When told to "take a faraway look," the cowboy was to look at the horizon where the sky meets the ground. By looking at the horizon, the cowboy could keep his bearings and balance while riding the twisting and turning bucking bronc. An airplane pilot has an instrument to assist him in pulling out of a tumbling turn, a false horizon instrument. The cowboy on the bucking bronc has to use the true distant horizon or at least the end of the rodeo area in order to keep his bearing while on the twisting bronc.

When the writer was younger, he and his brother broke horses to ride. There were many times that as the writer would mount a young quarter horse, he would hear, "Take a deep seat and a faraway look." It was only as the writer became more mature that he came to appreciate a different application of the saying—an application that could be used in handling some of the problems that developed in life.

There are times in one's life when a problem is about to "throw" a person. By "taking a deep seat," one prepares for a difficult ride. The preparation and expectation has immediate benefits in helping the person to ride it out. A person develops a mindset that he is going to be successful in riding out the problem because he has prepared himself mentally and physically for the task.

By "taking a faraway look," the individual must look to the future while handling the current problem of the day. If a person becomes immersed in the current problem, the loss of perspective of the future consequences may prove to be disastrous. An individual must keep his bearings. Becoming too involved with the problems of today, the actions needed for a successful tomorrow are ignored.

If a plane is tumbling among dense clouds, the pilot must rely upon his "false horizon" in order to bring his plane to an upright and a level flight. Taking the "faraway look" during the turmoil of a problem that is throwing one off balance (and possible unseating one from accomplishing a desired goal) will help an individual keep the proper future perspective needed for balance. For the bronc rider, "taking a faraway look" meant to look at the rodeo ground well ahead of him, the horizon, to keep an idea what was up and what was left or right as the bronc bucked.

All individuals have their broncs to ride or their problems to solve. Putting off getting down to the saddle on the bronc or avoiding handling the problem weakens the spirit. Do what is needed today! If the bronc bucks off the cowboy, he gets back on the bronc, if not a rodeo bucking horse. If a rodeo bronc throws the cowboy, he will ride another bronc in the next competition's go 'round. The first decision is to decide to ride, the second is to get on the bronc, and the third decision is to get back on if thrown off. *Take a deep seat and a faraway look.*

Why do we wait until tomorrow to do what needs to be done today?

SOME WE LOSE

Another favorite saying of the writer's cowboy father was "Some you win, some you lose, and in others, you're lucky to tie." This saying is popular among the professional rodeo cowboys who lose more often than they win. However, they will accept a tie as a neutral or an average, as splitting the go 'round money (such as splitting the third-place tie) is better than not receiving anything. The rodeo champions may win more often than they lose, but no one wins all the time.

So it is with life. In some things, individuals win, in some things they lose, and in other things, they feel fortunate to tie. Television and movie actors and actresses as well as professional athletes are a few of the individuals who feel they must win in order to measure their individual progress or see how they stand in some comparison to others of similar status. The problem is that in the TV shows or movies, because of retakes, the hero seldom fails, or if the hero does fail, he usually recovers at the end. Even the magazines that showplace exciting diets usually have to use the exceptional person who lost all of the weight, not the ordinary citizen who has to struggle to do so.

Some modern movies are now using this expected successful outcome to deliberately channel the hero's actions to a final failure to obtain a surprise ending. Sometimes to impact the audience, a favorite character dies or is severely hurt. In the old days of black-and-white movies, the good guys always wore white hats and the bad guys wore black hats. In those movies, good always won out. Real life throws the unexpected situations at unsuspecting individuals, and good does not always win out.

TV and magazine ads emphasize how easy it is to change, to improve, to feel better, to get better rates, get a better job, or to get more money or bonus points. Before-and-after pictures emphasize the effectiveness of the weight loss, or how much better the person can sleep or walk among grass and flowers without difficulty of allergies. The winners are always shown, and most commercials glide over the possible side effects.

Articles and professional TV guests and media stars all indicate how individuals can improve relationships with their spouses and/or children. Some, like psychologist Dr. Phil, are genuine, but even he will admit that a few of his efforts are failures. Because all of the hype is about how easy change is to do, the typical person is unprepared for the intensity of effort and length of time needed to implement the change.

One must be careful in approaching a challenge. Thinking one can fail may lead to actions to accomplish that anticipated goal. One should be confident and plan on succeeding. Don't allow a failure to cause extreme self-doubt. Don't allow the failure to avoid similar situations where one might fail again, and a critical concern, don't deny the outcome. Accept that a failure occurred, learn from it, and try again using what has been learned.

When a love relationship is broken, there is a loss. Sometimes one loses but then there is an opportunity to win someone else's love. Accept the loss but try again. In this example, a *tie* is dating without seeking a serious commitment. A *win* is finding someone who is better than the one who was lost. Remember emotions cloud rational thinking, and injured pride can prolong the pain of separation. Many individuals have lost a love relationship, either in high school or as an adult. Some win, some lose, and others are lucky just to tie. Accept the change and move forward.

Even multiple failures do not signify that there is no hope or no chance of being successful. History is full of examples of those who persevered and were eventually successful. One frequent example used is President Abraham Lincoln who failed many times in his political attempts but who eventually became successful and finished as one of the greatest of American presidents. The next chapter, "When a Puncher is Thrown" addresses the challenges of trying again. There is no win, lose, or tie if there is no attempt.

Why do we wait until tomorrow to do what needs to be done today?

WHEN A PUNCHER IS THROWN

The final saying of the writer's cowboy father that will be mentioned was "Never a bronc that couldn't be rode, and never a puncher who couldn't be thrown!" This cowboy saying was a very simple saying but it holds a wealth of wisdom. Too many of individuals believe that they must be successful in everything that they do, and even though they may be successful in ninety of the hundred things that they do, they want to be successful in all one hundred.

The really great coaches are those who can lead the team through losses. Any good coach can lead when the team is winning. Getting the team back up after a loss is both a skill and an art that most good coaches possess. Just as teams lose (or *get bucked off*, using the cowboy philosophy), those same teams must get ready to play again (or *mount up on a new bronc*, to continue the cowboy analogy), and the team members must believe that they can win.

In professional rodeo, a lot of the bronc riders are good riders, but there are some broncs that will buck off even the best of bareback riders or saddle bronc riders. All cowboys can be thrown and all can ride most of the broncs. Of course, there are some outlaw broncs that buck off the cowboys consistently.

As it is with teams and individuals who compete separately, nonathletes and noncowboys also have their own personal "broncs" to ride. It might be alcoholism, a severe illness, the loss of a loved one, a rebel teenager, a distant or ignoring spouse, hostile in-laws, money problems and so on. All of these and many other situations are difficult to "ride out." However, believing that one can "get back on and ride it out" is the first step to achieving that goal and to start positively toward accomplishing a needed change or modification of a situation.

A critical component of this saying, and thus of this concept, is that the person has to get back on the bronc. If a young cowboy is bucked off, he needs to mount up again as quickly as he can, especially the first few times that he is thrown from a horse so that he faces up to his fear of being bucked off again. By facing his fear, by immediately mounting up, he doesn't take time to imagine how he could have been hurt and allow his confidence to weaken in confrontation with what-ifs.

There is something extremely gratifying to face up to one's fear and overcoming that fear. Riding the bronc finally that had earlier thrown the cowboy five times allows him to face the next bronc that might throw him seven or eight times. But his belief that he can eventually ride the bronc comes from the successful facing of the times that he had been thrown before and had gotten back on.

In today's world, there are fewer cowboys, and the average person hasn't been on a horse. However, most people have been "thrown" or "knocked down," or suffered a loss, or made a mistake, or misjudged a situation, or in some way been unsuccessful. The lesson is that one must pick oneself up, get back on track to continue on with one's life, face up to the challenge and not give in to fear nor accept failure.

Sometimes one wins, sometimes one loses, and sometimes one ties. Many individuals can sometimes ride it out but sometimes one is thrown for a loss. If one is thrown, one should get back up and try again. All can be thrown at some time, but all can get back on again and again until there is the successful ride. Remember, "there never was a bronc that couldn't be rode and there never was a puncher who couldn't be throwed."

Why do we wait until tomorrow to do what needs to be done today?

WHEN THE MINUTES TURN INTO HOURS

For centuries, writers have indicated that time seems to slow in the presence of danger or while under a stressful state or while suffering. The song "The Wreck of the Edmund Fitzgerald" seem to sum up this concept best. The song is about a ship that is lost during a storm on one of the Great Lakes and was made popular by Gordon Lightfoot. In the song, the minutes appear to turn into hours.

All individuals have those times when the minutes seem to turn into hours. While waiting word of survivors of a plane crash, the return of a lost child, or the outcome of dangerous surgery, people have found that time seems to slow.

There is a tendency for a person to turn inward, to become self-contained, and to become introspective. There is a heightened feeling of isolation, even while being surrounded by friends and family. The apparent slow passage of time seems to increase the feeling of unreality, and thus the feeling of "being off-track" is heightened.

Since we are a society that revolves around the clock, we have an unconscious awareness of when events are to occur and a biological schedule that assists us in going through a day's cycle. When this is distorted, then the security of orientation in time and space is fragmented, and a feeling of drifting or floating occurs. For some, there is no conscious memory of the passage of time; and for some, time might be telescoped. The daily time markers that we all use to orient us to what we should be doing or where we should be may become stumbling blocks, or abandoned, or felt to be dimly out of reach.

Unless we have had some teenage memory of suffering through a lost teenage love, the sudden slowing of time is frightening if we are suffering through a tragedy expectation or a realized tragedy. If we are aware that such an experience is not unusual, that it is expected for many, then we can come to terms easier with the experience when it does occur. The unexpected and the unanticipated create the most difficult situations to surmount or to handle adequately.

If we realize that tragedy strikes all of us, then we need to begin now to set us a contingency plan to handle such an event. Just as we should plan how to get out of a burning home, or as we take first aid as a precautionary step, we should also plan how to handle tragic events. We could list those that we would want around as comforters. Who would be the person who could speak for the family if news reporters were to appear? Who could give the necessary information to authorities?

Would we need emergency money if we needed to travel to another location closer to an accident, or do we need places for relatives'to stay who are coming in to be by our sides to await the news? Who would be the objective third party that an individual could talk with about intense personal pain? Is there a neighbor, minister, relative, or even a professional that could be a sympathetic or objective ear?

It should be kept in mind that an impending tragedy could also upset an otherwise sensible relative or friend. A person needs a backup. However, some people deal with tragedy by seeking to be alone or by anger or hostility. Intense feelings are to be expected and many comments are made that should have been left unsaid.

Even when our worse fears become reality and even when we have a tentative plan to handle unanticipated tragedies, we sometimes forget to put the plan into action, or we react first. We may not be aware that we are not ourselves when awaiting bad news or while going through a tragedy. Awareness that we may not be our normal self is the first and foremost important step in working through this time. We must survive and live through this time.

Why do we wait until tomorrow to do what needs to be done today?

LOOKING FOR THE LOWER LIGHTS

When many of us think of setting goals, we think of some lofty or beyond-our-immediate-reach type of goals. We think of these goals as something beyond our reach or something that, in order to obtain, we need to look up. For centuries, man has looked up in the heavens to get direction and guidance as to where he was and where he needed to go. Poets and writers have also used this concept of putting goals upon a lofty pedestal so that man strives to reach upward to obtain his goals.

More realistically, most of us should look closer to earth to realize our goals or to get guidance. Instead of ridding the world of hunger, we could assist hungry people within our own community. Such a goal is not as lofty but is realistic and practical, and ultimately just as beneficial.

The old Christian hymn "Let the Lower Lights be Burning" illustrates the concept of looking for lower goals. The hymn was written after the passengers on a ship had reached a harbor safely, using the lower lights on the shores that were lower than the fog that had blanketed the harbor. This harbor was surrounded by treacherous reefs, and there was only a narrow entrance to the harbor. A lighthouse and the lights from the hillside houses of the rich were normally used at night for piloting in the large ships. One night, while running from an approaching storm, a ship approached the safe harbor only to find that a sudden and dense fog had blanketed out the beacon from the lighthouse and all the lights from the rich homes on the surrounding hills.

However, the captain and passengers discovered that below the fog there were reflected lights from the candles of the poor people who lived in the huts alongside the harbor. The ship was safely brought in by guiding in on the reflected candlelights from the low huts on shore. The hymn was then written to illustrate that God provides guidance from the lowly earth as well as from the lofty heavens.

In setting our goals, we really need both the lofty goals and the earthly goals. Many times the obtaining of the earthly goals are necessary before obtaining the higher and more lofty goals. With practice and confidence obtained from the successful completion of the lower and more practical goals, we can then raise our sights higher as we target the loftier goals.

Lofty goals are necessary, but practical and more earthly consideration are just as important. We need both the stars and the reflected candles on earth for guidance and motivation. We must remember to look also for the lower lights in seeking a safe ending for our own personal journeys.

Why do we wait until tomorrow to do what needs to be done today?

THE BLACK DOT

Most individuals know that too much of a good thing sometimes becomes a bad thing. Too much ice cream can cause an immediate stomach problem, and if continued for a longer time, may cause medical problems or at least, unwanted weight. We continue to do those things we like to do or make us feel good while we are doing it. We eat our favorite foods, pick out books by our favorite authors, listen to our favorite music, interact with our family and favorite friends, continue our favorite hobbies, and in general, we want to continue the happy life if we believe we are having a happy life. If we don't believe we have a happy life, we usually want to obtain a happy life.

Sometimes the reason we do not have a happy life is because we do have too much of a good thing. Consider the extremely rich, many of whom still are looking for happiness, even though many people believe that if they only had lots and lots of money, they would be happy. "Let me have all the money I need, and at least I will try and be happy" is often said with a grin. But money isn't everything, and having all of one's pleasures available doesn't bring happiness.

So many individuals want more. Instead of two cars, some people want another car, and a boat, and a four-wheeler. Instead of being comfortable in a three-bedroom house with four occupants, many want a four-bedroom house with an extra garage, four baths, and a large lawn with a large patio. Many wants and pleasures have a cost, most of which those who want them are not able to pay for them.

A frustration is sometimes the result of wanting something and not being able to obtain it. As we mature, we realize that all that we want is not going to be given to us. Most can come to terms with accepting limitations, or at least having a realistic view of what can be obtained. For some people, the continued frustration begins to build a bitterness, an anger sometimes, and for some, a feeling of depression.

Imagine or take out an eleven-and-a-half-inch sheet of white paper. In the center of that white paper, imagine or draw a circle around a dime. Fill in the circle with the black pen. Look at the sheet of paper and ask, "What do I see?" For most people, the answer is "a black dot." When told to look again, to give a complete description of what is seen, most will say a "black dot the size of a dime."

The complete description—the correct description—is "a white sheet of eight and a half inches in the center of which is drawn a black dot that is the size of a dime." Almost all individuals will only notice and thus describe what stands out in contrast to the white paper. After all, these people assume the white paper is a given. This is similar to an outlook that many individuals have who are frustrated with their lives, frustrated with what they don't have, and upset with that which they cannot obtain when they want it.

Most who look at the white sheet of paper and see only the "black dot" are focused on the black dot because of the extreme contrast. The black dot becomes the focal point, the focus of the gaze, and the white area around the dot is ignored. So it is with the unhappy individual who does not have all that he or she believes that he or she is entitled to have or should have; those who want more or want something that is not available now. They who are unhappy seem to focus their lives and their energies on the "black dot" and ignore the white page.

If the page of paper were to indicate a person's life, for most, the white portion would indicate the good things in their life. Good things would be living in the United States, having good health or having no handicaps, being loved by at least one person, having a family or having a satisfying job, a good involvement with a religious group and/or some organization that helps others, and so on. This is the white part of one's life—the important parts.

There are those who may want a single item so much that they ignore all of the good things in their life. They take them for granted and negatively focus on what they don't have. The "black dot," which is only a small part of the white paper, is only a small part of their lives. But by focusing on the "black dot" the white or the good part of their lives are forgotten, taken for granted and not appreciated. Maybe someone "should love you," but that person "does not have to love you." Love is part of the white part of life, the good part.

Sometimes embracing what one has and being comfortable with the acceptance will eventually assist in obtaining some or all that was wanted earlier. Remember, we are not talking about "needs." Needs are different than wants. One may need a car but want a Lexus. Too many people forget about their "haves" and focus on their "needs" or "wants." Sometimes when the "haves" are appreciated and acknowledged, the "needs" become fewer. Focusing on the black dot leads to a continued feeling of unhappiness and possible future depression.

As the Roman philosopher Epictetus remarked almost 2,000 years ago, "Men are disturbed not by things, but by the views which they take of them." This helps explain why some things bother some people significantly but are ignored by others. What view is taken of those things such as accidents, losses, recreational or work situations, family interactions, and many more? Would not a positive view be more effective in adopting to a change and an inner faith more conducive to living with a loss?

Why do we wait until tomorrow to do what needs to be done today?

SYSTEMS AND CYCLES

There is a tendency among many individuals to think either vertically or linearly. By *vertical thinking* is meant to be those people who think in terms of vertical alignment, like keeping a list, and because *B* follows *A*, and *C* follows *B*, then *D* must follow *C*. There is a certain comfort in knowing that things are in sequence and will follow the descending order or, in other cases, will ascend in a predictable manner. The *linear thinker* thinks in terms of a horizontal line, much like marching down a one-hundred-yard football field. After the five-yard line, there is the ten-yard line and then the twenty-yard line and the thirty. There is a natural sequence and, again, some predictability about consequences or results that occur from following that line of thinking.

Some will acknowledge that there are times that "leapfrogging" or bypassing the usual sequence is necessary, but the comfort level is disrupted. There may be some people who appear to be plodding along or who appear to be in a rut. Most creative thinkers do not follow the linear or vertical thinking mode of operation, although the most successful creative thinkers may utilize either the linear or vertical thinking in implementing their ideas.

Most people realize that there are cycles and systems that operate within the process of living. Individuals realize that there is the digestive system, the circulatory system, the nervous system, the reproductive system, and the other systems of living such as the memory system and the mental system. All of us are aware of the cycle of the seasons, the moon cycles, and other natural cycles that follow some type of order that directs the lives of many animals, insects, plants, and most types of water creatures.

A cycle may be a system, but not all systems are a cycle. Many cycles are closed and repeat themselves, such as the four seasons we experience in North America. Most systems are of the closed variety, such as the circulatory system or the nervous system. Not all agree as to whether the excretion or waste elimination system or the reproductive systems are closed or open.

Most things can be examined best by considering them as part of various interrelated systems. For instance, consider the universe as the largest system, the galaxy next, then our known solar system, next our planet earth, our North American continent, the United States, the state of Oklahoma, the county in which we live, and the community within the county. If a person lives within an apartment complex or a building where several nonrelated individuals or families live, then there is a further system of development.

However, there are more complex and interrelated social systems that impact us, not only socially but also mentally and physically. There is the work system, the church system, the club or organizational systems, political systems, neighborhoods, relatives, and, of course, the immediate family system. Most of these systems are fluid and are open; however, some are very closed or designed to be mostly closed. Fanatics or true believers or insecure individuals will often close these systems.

The major emphasis—the key—to the description of the systems theory is that each of these systems works within or have some impact on the other systems. From economical hard times impacting family structures to political decisions to mental nervousness to physical illness to the separation of families, moving to new locations with new neighbors and new schools or a new bunch of fellow workers, all of these systems— all—interact and impact each other. The impact may vary, the timing may change, and the outcomes could differ, but all of the systems, both external and internal, interact and in turn are impacted by the others.

Think of an old windup alarm clock. The clock is wound up, the alarm is set, but if one of the smallest interlocking wheels do not turn as designed, the entire system sets down. One wheel turns another, which turns two other wheels, which in turn turns other parts of the clock's mechanical, interlocking movements. One wheel's slowing will slow the entire clock's efficient operation.

In the system's concept, the view is circular, not linear or vertical. There are a number of elements and systems which loop back and tie in or adversely impact other operating systems. Instead of simple *A* causes *B* to happen, there may be intervening elements where the outcome is *C*, an unexpected outcome because of the interaction of other systems. An individual must consider all of the possible outcomes if planning a major change in one established or known system. For instance, if planning for a divorce, what are all of the factors and what systems will be impacted, both for the family unit as well as for the individuals within it?

Some years ago, the *butterfly effect* was popular to explain how a butterfly's wing flapping in Asia could cause weather patterns to be changed here in the United States. The idea was that there is no insignificant action and that all actions have a consequence if all of the various actions or consequences could be found and traced backwards to the original source. This type of linear thinking is really confusing when the systems theory concepts are applied.

For the individual, the process of thinking outside of the box, going beyond either linear or vertical thinking, incorporating the systems' concepts, and analyzing carefully any major change, is a necessity for planning that change. There are enough unseen consequences for the careful and slow thinker and consequences which include the creative and systematic thinker. When analyzing a potential major change, the linear or the vertical thinker who only thinks along those lines may face numerous consequences that may result in a disaster.

Why do we wait until tomorrow to do what needs to be done today?

STRESS: THE GOOD, THE BAD, THE UGLY

Every day, our bodies have to endure many different forms of physical stress ranging from polluted air, loud noises, too-tight clothing, junk food, sugar highs, health problems, and even lack of sleep. However, most times when the word *stress* is used, it is meant to be a mental or an emotional condition or pressure. Ironically, the emotional or mental stress problems can create physical health problems. No life is stress-free.

Stress expert Dr. Thomas S. Kepler indicated that "only 8 percent of a person's worries are legitimate." He said that 40 percent of the things worried about will never happen, 30 percent are over people's criticisms of the individual, 12 percent are over old decisions, and 10 percent are concerns about our health. People need to concentrate upon the remaining 8 percent. There is a continuum to stress along a pressure time line. From left to right on a continual line, there are three distinguishable stages: anxiety, tension, and eventually, stress.

One orientation platform from which to view stress is to organize it into one of three types of stress: good, bad, or ugly stress. Stress is an engineering term used to describe "a force with a tendency to distort." A number of things impact the different ways people manage stress. Some things can be support systems such as family, friends, coworkers or professional counselors, past experiences in handling similar stressful situations, and religious backgrounds. Another element is genetics, as some families have a history of stress-induced problems.

Dr. Chester Karrass, negotiation training expert and author of the popular 1995 book *Give and Take*, says that experiments confirm that emotions distort reality. People don't think clearly if they are emotionally involved. The individual's problems are intensified when the behaviors evolve out of the distorted pictures of reality impacted by the emotional feelings.

The good stress is positive stress. Good stress gives a person a type of energy charge, an adrenaline rush that can improve performance and give an emotional lift. Too much good stress then becomes the bad stress. Winning a multimillion-dollar lottery would be an example.

Bad stress is negative. Bad stress can cause blood pressure problems, an upset stomach, intense anxiety, irritable bowel problems, ulcers, an overwhelmed immune system, blood sugar problems, and heart disease. Stress hormones can lead to hypertension and to hardening of the arteries. Perceived stressful situations can be as serious a problem as actual stress (such as facing a masked robber). When the fight-or-flight adrenaline response is called upon too many times, the body's organs will suffer eventual damage.

Ugly stress develops when there is an overload of stress. Surprisingly, too much of the good stress, such as winning a multimillion-dollar lottery, can be as damaging as the bad stress, with a bad stress example being told that one has a progressing cancer. Stress, in varying degrees, is always with us.

There are hundreds of articles and books on how to handle stress and the sometimes-resulting depression. Changing jobs, getting a divorce, getting professional help and other types of stress resolutions may all be part of a systematic approach. After a medical examination to rule out physiological causes of anxiety or depression, or the feeling of being overwhelmed, these general four approaches to reducing stress are the mainstays of most authorities. The four main approaches for most people with most types of stress are:

(A) Exercise at least three times a week, although five times is best. The exercise needs to be at least thirty minutes of medium-plus intensity. Meditation, yoga, and other types of both mind and body relaxation practices are helpful, especially if done with physical exercise. Focused abdominal breathing that allows deep breaths to the lower stomach and then slowly released, while saying or thinking about breathing in calm and peace, and thinking that exhaling is getting rid of tension or stress, works with practice. Lying down in a quiet, dark area is best.

(B) Eat the right kind of foods. Many individuals have some degree of a food allergy to one or more types of food. Fatty foods and drive-in/takeout foods are too often the main food for busy people. Cutting back slowly and replacing with vegetables and nuts, along with less meat, is beneficial for stress carriers. A good multivitamin is needed, and some people need some additional minerals and vitamins as they approach physical life-changing situations. For quick relief of stress, dark chocolate has been shown to be of benefit if there are no diet problems.

(C) Begin the focus on helping others. When the focus is on positively helping others, there is less time to focus negatively on oneself. What is not totally understood is that when a person helps another, the person who is helping benefits as well. Church groups, cancer-prevention groups, children programs such as Big Brothers, various garden clubs or civic organizations, or even selecting to visit and help those in nursing homes or hospitals are just a few of the actions that will help others. Gifts and donations can be helpful but not as much benefit as physical involvement in helping others. This may not be true for all individuals.

(D) Set aside a scheduled me-time for doing things that are admittedly selfish. This could be as simple as thirty minutes of uninterrupted reading at a set schedule or a future vacation type of getaway. Visiting new places, trying new restaurants, a weekend shopping trip, a visit to family or out-of-town friends are a few examples of me-time. There are many other types of relaxing and different personal actions that satisfy one's inner and personal feeling that reinforces the thought "I deserve to be satisfied and happy." The key element is for one to be selfish for this instance, although it might be for only a short time.

There are a number of other very good methods for handling stress such as the *worry train*, whereby one puts the worries on various train cars and handle each car separately, or the *stopwatch* method of assigning so many minutes at a set time each day to worry and then, with lots of practice, ignore the mind's attempt to inject worry into the other daily life activities. The key to this is that worrying can become a habit that erodes one's happiness and confidence, and can create frustration and tension that can develop into illnesses. Most people can handle most of the normal stress that occurs most of the time if there is recognition that some action is needed. The key is to tackle the bad stress promptly with positive actions to reduce it.

Why do we wait until tomorrow to do what needs to be done today?

PERCEPTUAL FILTERS AS ROADBLOCKS

"To know thyself" was the philosopher Thales' (625–545 Bc) answer to the question, "What is the most difficult thing?" Two centuries later, Socrates echoed Thales' answer. Even today, with all of the recent scientific discoveries and the advancement of knowledge about the human body and modern man's social behaviors, most do not know themselves, and many do not want to know themselves. To know that one must improve is more challenging than ignoring any perceived need to do so. Also, as indicated in the "mirror" chapter, most people do not see themselves as needing to improve.

What we are not aware of is this: while we may believe that we see things are they really are, we really see things through a series of filters that alter, reduce, or distort the actual way we see things. How we view things through filters is impacted by and in turn develops how we feel about things and then believe about things. The phrase "Beauty is in the eye of the beholder," or "Love is blind" or "A starving man doesn't see bad food," are only a few illustrations of how we see things through a filter. These filters may change with experiences, education, maturity, occupations, or a significant lifestyle change such as military service. Marriage and becoming a parent also create new filters and may change other filters previously in place.

Most people think of filters as an oil filter in a car or an air-conditioner filter, or some other type. Sunglasses are a filter as they reduce the glare and the sun's rays. Most filters reduce something (the sun's brightness) or removes something, such as dust particles from the air (A/C filter) or a car's oil filter that removes metal engine parts or dirt from the oil.the oil.

Another example is this: Just as a coffee filter allows the water to pass through but keeps out the coffee grounds, our thoughts pass through similar "mental filters" that change our perceptions in much the same way as clear water is poured into the coffee pot and emerges as dark coffee. The mental filters are as different for people as are fingerprints. Most miscommunications can be blamed in part of the different filtering processes that form the perceptions between the communicators.

There are many, many filters, most of which are not known to a person, and most times are not recognized by others. For instance, an attitude of prejudice developed by childhood modeling of parents is not recognized as a filter by either the individual or by the family members for which such an attitude is expected and rewarded. Even the foods and beverages that one chooses may go through a series filters. A filter, such as a bad experience filter (throwing up a bad food item) or a perceived good filter, such as adhering to the popular commercials or what is "cool" with the peer group "can periodically be changed." Most dislikes and likes evolve from filters.

Most individuals know that a stimulus elicits a response. S equals R is taught in schools and by parents. An action has a response. Most think that this is the entire equation. In between the stimulus and the response is the filter that directs or chooses the response. Some stimuli, such as pain or smell or taste or noise react with a response from the old part of the brain, sometimes called the *lizard brain*. This is the "older" brain that allowed earlier man to survive by kicking in the adrenaline, physical response to danger, commonly called the flight-or-fight response. With training, some of these SR natural responses can be modified. One should keep in mind that not every stimulus goes through a filter before a response is made, but almost all choice responses do, even though a person is not conscious of it.

Just a few of the filters will be listed here. In an earlier chapter, there was discussion of the external versus the internal locus of control. This is perhaps the most critical mental filter that alters perceptions. A few chapters from now, the "OK corral attitude or mental set" perceptual filters are listed. How we look, i.e., visually see an item and still disagree as to what it really "looks like" is also discussed later. The explanations of problems in seeing what others see and believe and the problems that result from misperceptions are common threads among all of the chapters.

One type of filter is the type-A or the type-B personality filter. The type-A personality has an intense drive to work hard and to achieve. The type-A person pursues a self-serving process and will spend long hours to achieve success, sometimes sacrificing the needs or desires of others. The type-B personality is more patient; more inclined to work together, be cooperative and flexible. There is a tendency by the type-B person to share and to be a team player instead of a team leader. Other's needs and time are considered. If a line were drawn as a continuum, with type A on end and type B on the other, one could envision a dictator on one end and a likeable, unemployed-but-happy individual on the other.

Other listed early-developed filters are: single-parent families, level of religious activities of the family, number of brothers and sisters, closeness of significant relatives such as grandparents, economic levels, home locations, occupations of parents (coal miners versus farmers versus clerical workers versus military families, etc.), and a number of other social and physical elements. Mistreatment, reactions to the color of skin, peer problems, medical problems and a host of other things all are meshed into the filtering system held by others. These filters may change and improve or become more entrenched as an individual has new experiences and as the individual ages. The comments on Maslow's need hierarchy in chapter 4 need to be reviewed.

Some filters are stronger than others. Some filters are triggered by stimulus words. Some filters act in concert with others or when triggered, will trigger an unintentional filter. Filters can be feelings, beliefs, values, past experiences, intrinsic goals, training, education, and any number of other causes. After viewing a horror movie, the sounds of the night may be perceived differently.

What an individual can do is try to understand why he believes or behaves in the ways that he does. Are those thoughts the ones he wants? Are his behaviors the ones he feels most comfortable with? Does he need to change? Which filters give him inaccurate information? It was Aldous Huxley who said, "There are things known and there are things unknown, and in between are the doors of perception." Filters alter our knowledge and our perceptions of reality.

Why do we wait until tomorrow to do what needs to be done today?

THE THERMOMETER PERSON

A number of years ago, an individual wrote that there are two basic divisions of people—those who control circumstances and those who allow circumstances to control them. Those people who control circumstances he called thermostat people. Those who allow circumstances to control their lives he called thermometer people.

He explained that a thermostat controls the temperature within a room. If it is too cool, the thermostat turns on the heat. If the room is too hot, the thermostat turns on the air conditioning. In other words, the temperature of the room is controlled by the thermostat. In this instance, the circumstance of the room's interior temperature is controlled by the thermostat.

By contrast, the thermometer merely reflects the temperature of the room. If the room is too hot, the thermometer merely reflects the high temperature. If the room begins to become too cool, again the thermometer only is able to reflect the current temperature. In other words, in this example, the circumstance (the temperature) controls the thermometer. The thermometer person reflects the main expectations of society or the behaviors of the group about him or her. This person merely follows the dictates of the majority. If most people are getting a tattoo, then he or she will get one. If the popular movie star doesn't shave, neither will the thermometer man. If the popular music diva wears eight-inch heels while night clubbing, so will the thermometer woman.

The thermostat man or woman doesn't always exert control on those people around them. They do, however, control their thoughts and feelings and behaviors in response to the circumstances. Most heroes are thermostat individuals as are most leaders. The thermometer individual follows and takes comfort in the safety of numbers, i.e., everybody is doing it. These individuals are easily manipulated by the thermostat people, and the thermometer individuals are easy marks for commercials. Most thermometer people want to be liked and accepted. Also, many times they will show their feelings and in turn, will have their feelings hurt more easily.

A caution: there is no absolute thermostat or thermometer individual. There is a mixture of both in most people. The difference is in percentage of thermometer actions compared to those which are considered thermostat actions. If a person functions at least 70 percent of the time in one or the other of the two behavioral patterns, then the person is presumed to be a thermometer or a thermostat person.

There are some individuals who can easily switch from one to the other, from a thermostat person in one environment to a thermometer person in another environment. An example of switching areas might be a work environment versus the home/parent environment or the church environment or a recreational environment. There is also a time line. A new recruit may copy the attitudes and actions of the old timers but eventually a true thermostat will exert his or her own personality in the work situation.

The military is thought to want their top officers to be thermostat people but want the rank and file enlistees to be thermometer people—individuals who will follow orders and follow the written and unwritten military codes of behavior. Most organizations that rely upon teamwork want the basically thermometer individual because of this group's tendency to follow directions, work cooperatively, maintain order, and endure shared hardships and disappointments.

Most of the thermostat people are happier than the thermometer people, as the thermostat people have only to satisfy themselves. Many times the thermometer people are trying to satisfy others and may be anxious and worried that they are not being good enough. An individual needs to do a self-analysis and determine if he or she is a thermostat or thermometer person, most of the time. Once a determination is made, a choice is then possible as to which type of individual that one wants to become.

Why do we wait until tomorrow to do what needs to be done today?

BEING BLIND AND NOT "SEEING"

In a poem titled *"The Blind Men and the Elephant,"* written by John Godfrey Saxe, the story is told of six blind men who lived in India. These six blind men decided to see an elephant, but as they were blind, each had to "see" the elephant with his hands. In the poem, each of the six men happened to place his hands upon a different part of the elephant. Each of the six men begin to describe what the elephant "looked like" according to what the blind man had felt with his hands as his hands had been acting as his eyes.

One man felt the trunk of the elephant and said the elephant was like a snake. Another felt the side of the elephant and said the elephant was a wall. The third man grabbed the tail and said the elephant was like a rope. One blind man felt one of the legs and said the elephant was like a tree trunk. Another felt the tusk and said the elephant was like a spear. The last man felt the elephant's large ear and said the elephant was like a fan.

Each man had felt only a part of the elephant with his hands and each had described what he thought the elephant "looked like" from using his hands to feel the elephant. The six men begin to argue about who was right. What did the elephant look like?

The concluding lines of the poem are these:

> The six good men of Indostand
> Argued loud and long,
> Each was partially in the right,
> But all were in the wrong.

What the writer said was that each of the blind men was correct in what each saw with his hands, but each saw only a portion of the elephant. Each was partially right in what he saw, but all were wrong in thinking how the entire elephant looked. So it is with some individuals who try to see a situation but who have limited vision or experience, or who are blind with anger or jealousy, or are scared or prejudiced, etc. People can become blind and see what they want to see or expect to see or even see things in terms of their own needs or experiences.

There can be conditioned responses and canned answers because of the limiting of the total picture projected by the "seeing" of blind hands. Writers use terms like "blindly in love" or "he follows blindly" to indicate a mental blindness that handicaps others, like the physical blindness handicapped the six good men of India. The difficulty is not knowing what "blind spots" individuals might have. To avoid being one of the blind men, individuals need to try to keep at least one eye open to see the entire picture, to see both sides, and to be aware of differences that might be correct.

Why do we wait until tomorrow to do what needs to be done today?

WHAT IS THIS?

When starting this chapter, stop and look at the illustration below or at the end of the CD. If driving, do not look at the illustration unless stopped. Look at the animal that is shown and say aloud what the animal appears to represent.

Illustraion 3

If the answer given was a *rabbit*, the eyes probably went from right to left as the eyes processed the image and the mind gave meaning to what was viewed. If the answer given was a *duck*, then the eyes probably processed the image from left to right. If the rabbit's nose and then the ears were seen, the rabbit image was processed. If the bill (the blunt ears on the rabbit version) on the left was seen first and then the eye and head, the image was seen as a duck.

The perception of the animal could be either the rabbit or the duck. This is an ambiguity which means that there are two ways of reading the presentation of the sense (vision), and that both could be right. Perception could be said to be made up of "memories as well as sensations." The principles of association and recall impact the perception as well. If no memory exists of either experience or obtained knowledge from school or the shared verbal experiences of others, then a perception is possibly inaccurate. For instance, the American language is difficult to learn for those individuals who grew up with a foreign language as their early communication. American slang expressions or words that sound the same but mean different things (such as too, to, or two) are examples.

Another problem exists where there is conflict between one generation and another over such items as tattoos, ear or nose piercing, clothing, drinking, friend choices, dating conduct, and so on. Multimedia influences and shifting values shade perceptions as well as religious beliefs, and various social events such as divorce or other losses also develop rifts among perceptions. Remember the perception of either a duck or a rabbit illustration when two people look at the same thing but may see something different. It is reasonable to believe then that degrees of perception differences on other things could be numerous.

Sometimes, there is not a conscious left-to-right or right-to-left processing of the duck/rabbit illustration. There could be a gestalt view, or a total picture seen as a whole and then processed. In either instance, if only one view was seen, the individual processing the image is only obtaining half of the possibilities. If there is a quick, one-second request for an answer, most only see one image. But then, when the image is examined for discussion, most stay with their original decision as to whether it was a rabbit or a duck. A frequent comment made is, "if you really tried hard to see it the other way, I guess you can, but it really looks most like..." or a defensive comment like "the image really doesn't look like either a rabbit or a duck."

No one wants to be wrong. Few like to be tricked. Most people stay with their first impression. But imagine if this image were to be shown to a number of individuals who were told to write down the favorite foods and the most prevailing behaviors of the animal that they "saw" in the illustration. Individuals will argue for how they believe their animal will behave. "Swim in the water, no way. He'll run and jump, not fly," and other comments will continue until someone clears the confusion about which of the two different animals is being discussed.

If a simple image can cause people confusion because of what their eyes interpreted, think of the confusion and the causes of many arguments when abstract subjects, emotions, or topics are discussed. Individuals may process the same data in different ways. Most people want their friends (and may choose them so) because they view situations or events or ideas or concepts the same way. Religious groups, political groups, coffee groups, clubs/organizations, sports fans, various teams, and so on are usually made up of individuals who view things and think about things, for the most part, in a similar manner.

When one person is arguing from a logic point of view (in his or her opinion) the argument can become unsolvable when the other person is arguing from an emotional point of view. The true purpose of an argument is to clarify and resolve a difference between at least two individuals. When different views are held, and when those views become rigid, there is usually no progress unless at least one person considers the other's view. Being able to see both sides or a different viewpoint does not mean the individual agrees with that different viewpoint, but there is an acknowledgment that the person does see it differently.

The wrong or unacceptable viewpoint may be presented, like many of the arguments between parents and their teenagers or between a husband and a wife. When no one gives ground, more understanding is lost and postponement, in most cases, may result in hardened emotions and resentment. What is truly unfortunate is that many arguments begin because of simple mistakes in interpreting (seeing the image) correctly the cause of the discomfort or the real reason for the difference. The perception varies between the two individuals, and both may be only half right. Recognizing that there is another view is not the same as accepting that view.

Why do we wait until tomorrow to do what needs to be done today?

THE HOT POTATO GAME

Too many individuals are uncomfortable with accepting responsibility, either for their own actions or for the actions of those over whom they have control or influence. Some will distant themselves by a physical separation, such as moving to a different neighborhood or community, or moving to a different department or even to a different company. Changing employment to a less-demanding position is often done when the responsibility begins to weigh heavy on the person's mind and feelings.

Avoidance of the individual or of the situation, or a failure to face up to the problem is typical. Some people develop the habit of engaging in the "hot potato" game of passing the problem on to someone else. Some are extremely adept at passing the hot potatoes that come their way and rarely are found out by others. Most can get by occasionally with passing it on up to the boss but there is a point where one must assume the level of responsibility inherent in the job that he is doing.

More difficult to explain are the interrelationships in which the hot potato is passed from one to another, often being tossed back to the original passer without the item being "cooled" or diminished. Parents are often involved in this passing the hot potato game when the hot potato item is discipline. "You're the father. You handle your unruly teenage son," or "You're the mom, you talk to her about boys and their behaviors," and so on.

Sometimes the parents work together to toss the hot potato to another party—the minister or the school principal or another family member. This is especially true with children's misbehavior or attitude. "He won't listen to us. He likes playing football, so coach, can you...?" or "You're a minister and you see this all the time. Can you help us with...?"

The professional hot potato tosser knows that as the hot potato is tossed about, it begins to cool. He knows that time may cool the hot potato problem, so he is in no hurry to solve the problem. He feels time is on his side, so many times he puts off a decision or avoids taking the needed action. Many of the more experienced hot potato tossers become successful in passing the blame for the delay (or the blame for failure to resolve the problem) to one of the other receivers of the tossed hot potato.

Sometimes it is the innocent individual who unthinkingly catches the tossed hot potato who is hurt emotionally or who has the blame for the mishap applied to him. The other hot potato tossers are relieved that they weren't burnt or blamed for mishandling or not handling the hot issue. The habit of avoidance is a costly habit and usually ends badly for the person utilizing that process to resolve problem situations. Sometimes it is in the receiver's best interest to drop the passed hot potato.

Why do we wait until tomorrow to do what needs to be done today?

THE OK CORRAL FILTER

Most of us have an unconscious mental set or an unconscious attitude from which we may use, most times, in "viewing others." Based on the ideas of transactional analysis psychology presented by Dr. Eric Berne's 1960s bestseller book, *Games People Play*, Dr. Thomas Harris, in his 1967 book, "*I'm OK, You're OK*" advances the belief that we hold four mental sets or attitudes from which or through which we view or see others. This view that we hold establishes an attitude with which we interact with other people. This author would add that these mental sets or attitudes create a filter through, which we view and thus interpret communication and relationships.

The central core of his book is that we each behave toward other people based upon whichever attitude that we hold toward these people. Dr. Harris believes that there are four (4) basic "mental sets" from which we view or see others which develop into the four basic attitudes. There are three negative attitudes and one positive attitude. Attitudes can be seen as filters. Remember, the purpose of any filter is to reduce or trap some element. A *Dennis the Menace* cartoon had the caption "Imagination is what lets you remember things that never happened."

The term "corral" is used to illustrate that three of the negative attitudes limit or corral any effective communication or interaction with others. A person needs to either mentally or physically draw a box for visual purposes. Each side of the box represents one side of the "OK corral." Three sides of the corral are fixed, and only the fourth side is a gate that opens up effective communication and interaction.

The first OK corral side is the attitude or mental set of "*I'm OK...You're Not OK.*" In this instance, the individual feels that he is okay, that he is a good person who is successful in working his way through life and solving the problems that develop. However, all other people or most other people are not okay, and their messed-up lives are a result of not believing or behaving the way that he does. This belief maintains an "I am right and they are wrong" orientation. Many times, the blame for this person's mistakes is placed on some successful other person.

The second OK corral side is the attitude or mental set of "*I'm Not OK...You're OK.*" This person has a very low self-esteem. The beginnings of the feelings of low self-worth may begin within the family or within the schools. An older sibling may receive all of the praise, or the school peer group rejects acceptance of the individual. Sometimes a physical problem such as being too fat, too ugly, or being handicapped is a cause. Poverty and race are other factors that some believe or even accept that those persons are not as okay as others. Others are seen as okay, and the individual who feels like he is not okay wants to be like those who are.

The third OK corral side is the attitude or mental set of *"I'm Not OK...You're Not OK."* This is a more desperate attitude because there is not an apparent better situation or relief, or even a better goal that is available. The individual is unhappy and believes that everyone else is just as unhappy as he is. He believes that everyone thinks as he thinks, and he thinks in negative terms. Feelings of depression and hopelessness, bad moods and mood swings, temper outbursts and avoidance of responsibility for one's behavior may be part of the mixture and may surface without any apparent reason. He uses a trial-and-error method to try to find meaning.

It is only the fourth side, the gate side, of the OK corral that opens up effective communication and develops needed relationships. The gate side of the OK corral is the attitude or mental set of *"I'm OK... You're OK."* This is the only healthy attitude or mental set from which to view life and from which to act in a responsible manner. This individual believes that he and all other people are okay. People may be odd, people may do things differently, but what they do is sufficient for them and as such, okay. It does not mean that an individual's bad behavior is okay or whose actions that hurt someone else are okay. It is the belief that individuals have the ability to be okay or to act appropriately.

Some individuals—an extreme example might be criminals—may not act appropriately, but they could, or at least at one time, have made a different choice. The okay individual believes in the potential goodness in himself and in others. The communication is direct and frank and nonthreatening. There is warmth and acceptance of diverse views and acceptance of a variety of different behaviors and responses as long as none of the behaviors harm others.

The "I'm okay and you are okay" mental set or attitude is the mentally healthy point of view and, as mentioned in the preceding paragraph, the most effective in developing successful interrelationships with others. It is okay to love and to be loved. One is worthy and others are also worthy although they may be different. Tolerance and acceptance of other individuals' differences and weaknesses are part of this mental set or attitude. Society needs this belief.

Why do we wait until tomorrow to do what needs to be done today?

LIMITED WORDS, LIMITED EXPRESSIONS

A study at an Eastern university some twenty years ago or more indicated that 80 percent of our conversation involved only some four-hundred-plus words. The word "I" was in the top five most used words. In today's text messaging and computer-driven world, the number and frequency of words or word shortcuts (*UR* for "you are") would change that study. With the increasing loss of face-to-face type of communications, misperceptions are destined to increase. And, as Anthony J. Cedoline said in 1982, "No manager devotes effort to proving himself wrong." Similarly, individuals can easily make wrong impressions from misperceptions which are seldom corrected and which may not be known. Once known, more energy and effort is required to change the mistake than to let it be.

As humans, we communicate better than any of the other animals. We communicate the best with our expressed words (in our native language) and our facial expressions. Our nonverbal facial expressions come first, next is body language, then sign language and finally, verbal expression. Modern expression is complicated and often layered.

The American English language is confusing to most visitors from other countries. We have words that sound alike but have different meanings like "to" or "too" or "two." We have words that sound the same but are different in meaning. We have words that mean different things depending on how the word is used in context of the sentence. Then we have slang words which change constantly.

Then today, in this technologically driven modern world, we have new words being coined each month. Text messaging has added new words, messed up the spelling and sentence diagrams with which the older generations are familiar. Commercials and political slogans impact the language as well, and subtle references to TV shows or movies slip in to modify the older meaning of some vocabulary words. Finally, the constant including of many formally vulgar words, cuss words, and impolite expressions in street talk, rap songs, TV shows and movies limit the creative expression and conversations that were welcomed by earlier generations and were a sign of a good education and a "proper upbringing."

It has been said that the six most important words are "I admit I made a mistake." The three most important words are "I love you," and the most important word is "we" or, as some believe, "please" is the single most important word. It is not only what is said, but how it is said, and the accompanying facial expression must mirror the intent of the words.

Some believe that the best communicators are like the best comedians. Imitators cannot say the same thing in the same way as a very good communicator; and while many can repeat a joke that a good comedian used and which received a good laugh, those repeating the joke may have the joke fall flat. The best actors and actresses have that intangible something that makes their acting look natural and their communication believable.

Most of us need to improve the methods we use to communicate to avoid misunderstandings. We need to avoid tired expressions, same old slang, vulgar or cuss words, bad grammar and non-face-to-face visiting. We need to avoid the "going through the motions" of communicating where the dialogue is worn out, the language is repetitive, and no one is listening because the other is tuned out, or the listener is busy thinking of what he or she is going to communicate next.

Why do we wait until tomorrow to do what needs to be done today?

THE ALDIS LAMP

The Aldis lamp was used for communication by the British Royal Navy in the late 19th century and is still used today for secure communications when radio silence is needed or if radio transmissions are not available. Although there are various types, the basic principle is a bright light that can alternately be shown or darkened, allowing signals to be transmitted and received, usually in Morse code. This works best at night and can be seen from a ship or from land to the ocean's horizon.

For the Aldis lamp to work, there has to be a sender and a receiver, both of whom know the signals or code being used. There is a very narrow line of sight between the two communicators, and training is needed. In practice, it is sometimes possible to illuminate cloud bases, both during the day and especially at night for communications over the horizon. Modern armed forces usually use the infrared spectrum (IR) to avoid easy detection. Most airports have signal lamps in their traffic control towers as a backup device in case of an aircraft's radio failure.

While the Aldis is functional in today's armed forces and as backup for airplanes, most of the modern communications are by telephone, cell phone, television, or various radio and computer bands. Focused beams to general broadcast signals allow a limited or major network coverage. Yet all of these communication devices have a weakness. Wireless communications, and even television presentations to a viewer, both lack the subtle and personal communication that goes beyond just what is being said and heard between two people face to face, especially if the two are close.

Husbands and wives and former partners, lovers, parents and children, and good friends are the basic groups that can communicate more than the words that are expressed. Stressful events such as combat teamwork, law enforcement partners and fire department personnel are some examples of enhanced communication. To a lesser extent, prison confinement, gang involvement, and teen peer pressure groups may also be developers of a shared communication.

This chapter is focused on the husband/wife and the parent/child communicators, the two which should have the highest percentage of true communication of thoughts and feelings. Yet one of the most common expressions of miscommunication among parents and teenagers and husbands and wives is the phrase "You don't understand me!"

There are a variety of reasons, but the focus will be on the Aldis lamp illustration. If an analysis of the communication-process failures of couples and parents and children were to be made, one or more of the suggestions below could be an explanation as to a cause.

First, there are distracters (such as TV or radios in the background) or other people who are either present or walking about. These distracters are significantly interferers.

Secondly, there is no eye-to-eye contact, especially for the intimate or we-love-each-other zone of two to three feet between two individuals. It is felt that the best communication is between two individuals, one to one. Much less effective communication is one to one with another individual listening. Driving a vehicle while talking to another is one of the worst ways to communicate. This is because there is seldom meaningful eye-to-eye contact, and there are too many distractions for both. Focus is lost and miscommunication often results. Having said that, some couples and parents and teenagers are successful in resolving some conflicts while driving. More individuals are successful in parking the car and talking while trying to communicate important information and feelings.

Third, one or both of the communicators focus only on what is said—only the literal meaning—and pay little or no attention to the unspoken elements of communication such as facial expressions, inflections of the voice, the pauses, the hidden stressed word or phrase, and the most critical part of eye-to-eye communication, the unspoken language of the eye.

Fourth, one or both of the communicators begin the conversation with predetermined ideas about what the conversation will be, or having a compartment of ready-to-use "zappers" to use at a later time, or an I'm-getting-this-off-my–chest-first orientation. *Telling someone* is not the type of communication that is being discussed. *Sharing with someone* and having that someone share back the thoughts and feelings with trust and belief that both are together, or desire to be together, is the goal. When together on the goal, the gain is greater understanding with a more truthful and deeper communication.

Fifth, the location and timing are critical factors. Some people prefer the kitchen or the dining room table, sometimes eating a snack while involved in the needed communication. Some prefer the bed, but propped up, side to side, to allow eye-to-eye within the intimate zone. Physical discomforts can interfere if the conversation becomes long. Sometimes the den or sofa, or maybe a neutral site such as the patio or even a park bench is best (if no distractions).

Timing is critical and too many times the needed communication is put off until one or the other feels that "the time has come," and there are no preparations and the other individual feels that an ambush has occurred. Then, the perceived attacker is facing a defensive respondent. If either of the individuals are facing a significant event in the near future, for instance a high school event the next day or meeting with the manager the next morning, the timing is wrong. Attempting to communicate with someone who is strained emotionally, such as (a) being depressed, (b) extremely tired from work, (c) emotionally exhausted from the loss of a friend or relative, or (d) one who has just received bad medical or financial news, is rarely successful.

Sixth, a person should not push or demand that an understanding of what either is trying to communicate has to occur. Sometimes understanding evolves from reflection and time and distance from the intensity of deep emotions. "Let both of us think some more about this and get together again to try to work this out!" is one way of ending a frustrating failure to adequately communicate either person's thoughts and feelings. Sometimes it will take a number of attempts to establish that desired and needed communication link.

An individual who is sincerely interested in trying to understand another must have patience, the ability to see things from the other person's point of view, the persistence to continue, and a realization of the viewpoint of the other, no matter how personally painful it might be or how hurtful it is to the other (drug usage is an example) for purposes of the initial communication. An individual doesn't have to agree with that viewpoint, but if person 1 cannot agree to listen to person 2's view, how then could person 2 feel that he should accept person 1's view? After all, communication is a sharing process and often all individuals may feel some discomfort.

Why do we wait until tomorrow to do what needs to be done today?

THE WHITE CARD AND THE CUBE

This particular chapter needs the reader's or listener's complete attention. If driving a car, it is suggested that listening to this portion may be distracting. This chapter is more meaningful if two suggestions are followed: (1) involve another person and (2) have the mentioned materials available. While imagining the sequencing of the descriptions can be accomplished, the most meaningful and the longer memory of these items are best served by physical involvement, again with another person.

One should choose a "white card," some 3 inches by 5 inches or a very thick piece of white paper that is cut similar to the size above. The thick piece of paper should not allow any writing on one side to be "viewed through" by someone looking at the opposite side. If two people are involved, one person can write "me" on one side and "you" on the other. One's name can be written on one side and the other's name written on the other side. Any two combinations of items can be listed as long as they are different. For example, two religions, two vacation areas, two friends, books or movies, two political parties, and many other combinations lend themselves to being viewed and discussed in this manner.

Person 1 can hold up the card between the two, in this example, having the portion of the card saying "me" facing the presenter and with the card side saying "you" facing the other person. It is more dramatic if the other person doesn't see what is written on either side by the presenter. The card is held up and the presenter asks, "What do you see?" Almost all will say "you." The presenter says, "Are you sure that is what is written on the card?" After the response, the next comment by the presenter can be "Well, I see something different," or "I see the word 'me,'" or "You're wrong. I see the word 'me.'"

The presenter flips the card so that the opposite person then sees "me" written on the card and again asks "What do you see?" When the answer is given, the presenter can say, "No. The card says 'you,'" or some similar comment. Then the critical questions are asked, "Why are we seeing different words? After all, we are looking at the same card," and/or "we are examining the same situation," or "we are both looking at the same thing and we should see it the same way."

Some individuals will quickly indicate that there are two sides to the card. The presenter should immediately indicate that this is the correct answer. For others, there may be a slower realization. The presenter then explains that often individuals look at the same situation but see it differently, just as each has seen a different side of the card.

For a more effective demonstration, before starting this exercise, place two chairs facing each other, with the card or paper with the two items already completed, out of sight of the viewer. Go through the above steps for the presentation. Then when the question is asked, the second most important question, "How can we see the other person's point of view?" the presenter moves his chair alongside that of the other viewer, holding up one side or the other so that both see the same side at the same time.

The presenter can say "This is the only way we can begin to see what the other person sees…" or "…what is most relevant" or "…most needed" or "…favored," or whatever defining difference(s) there are between the two different views or concepts. Together, all look at each view and listen to the explanation as to why that view is held.

An alternate method is for the presenter to move the card back and to one side so that the presenter can see the side shown to the other person, i.e., both are looking at the same side at the same time. Likewise, flip the card so that the other individual is seeing what the presenter had originally seen, again both looking at the same view. Until there is realization that there are two valid viewpoints, there can be no progress in resolving differences or a mutual agreement as to which to choose. Indicating that there is another side does not equate with accepting it.

A person who indicates that he recognizes the different view does not and should not imply acceptance of that view. For instance, a mother discussing why her teenager believes that using drugs are okay doesn't have to agree with that view. However, the mother needs to realize that peer pressure or drug dependence is reinforcing her teenager's different view. It is critical that the teenager also understands why the mother has her views (that it is against the law is a moot point).

The cube or a small rectangle of wood or some six-sided object can be used to illustrate a number of different views or different elements such as time elements (now, tomorrow, next week, next year, whenever, or never), vacation spots (reasons for and against choosing one), or for comparisons of items like religions, books, plays, music, etc. Each side can be used for another view. A taped paper can be removed to allow multiple views. A rubber ball can be effectively used if care is taken to sufficiently separate the different views.

Finally, a cube or a small rectangle piece of wood can be painted different colors on each of the six sides—red, black, white, yellow, blue, or orange, or some other color. The point is that each of these may "look differently" because of the color, but if the paint is scraped off, the wood that is underneath is the same for each of the painted sides.

There are a lot of variations that can be used to illustrate differences and ways to assist in working out solutions. Almost all involve the perceptions, the previous experiences, and the feeling of comfort or security of focusing on a particular view. Remember, sometimes handling the items (card or wood block) assist in the retention of the suggestions or points made because some 10 percent of individuals learn best through tactile or a physical handling of the item. For others, hearing the different views is the method best for their learning.

Why do we wait until tomorrow to do what needs to be done today?

PORTRAITS VERSUS PHOTOGRAPHY

Most individuals realize that a portrait of a person is different than a picture made of the same person. The picture is a snapshot, at that point in time, of a person whereas the portrait is developed over a period of time. The picture is real whereas the portrait is influenced by the hand and the mind and the impression desired by the artist. It is true that some artists try to capture the very likeness of the individual being painted.

It is also true that with today's excellent photographers, with studio lighting, background softening, and "camera shopping," a picture can come close to an approximation of a painted portrait. Still most artists leave something of how they "see" a person when representing that individual in a painting. The old portrait masterpieces capture something in their portrayal of someone that is difficult to describe.

It can be said that when individuals look at someone they love, they are seeing that person as a portrait, not as a picture. Love sees things in a rose-colored and soft world, not the harsh lines of even a colored photograph. But as the portrait fades, so does the depth of love.

Most individuals want to see the world as photographs but want to feel the world as a portrait. There are a number, however, who are not flexible and lock in one perception or view, such as the portrait and continually see or view the world through that perspective. It is not truly a practical versus a romantic view or orientation because most of us are some of each, but we generally have more of one kind of view than the other. Many could benefit from changing the boundaries of the two.

How individuals view another person is critical because the view held often dictates the type of behavioral responses that individuals make to that person. Many individuals are very adept at hiding their real emotions and are able to act differently than what they feel. Sometimes there are lapses. An individual who likes or dislikes another person usually has a range or a gauge that is used to measure or limit the amount of feelings or behaviors that are expressed or made evident. Proximity, past experiences, and social practices all influence the likes and dislikes.

The same actions are interpreted differently if viewed from a "portrait" frame of reference versus a "picture" frame of reference. Parents forgive or overlook those behaviors of their children that would invoke criticism or correction if incurred by someone else's children. The portrait frame of viewing softens the realistic view of others. The greater the love, the more suspect the view becomes. This doesn't mean individuals should not love; rather, individuals should understand why some people may see others in a different light or frame or view, and, whose view may be more accurate or realistic. Strong emotions color the view.

Why do we wait until tomorrow to do what needs to be done today?

WHEN THE MIND IS TRICKED

The human eye is exceptional. At night, a person with excellent vision can spot a lit candle some fourteen miles away. It can distinguish differences among some five hundred shades of gray. However, seeing or perceiving or making sense of what is seen is a function of the brain. The brain has to be able to tell the difference between the foreground and the background and tell lines from edges. Examples have already been illustrated to show how the eyes can be tricked and how the brain can misinterpret the input from the eyes. Which soldier is tallest?

If listening while driving, wait until it is safe to examine the illustration that is shown on the next page or shown at the end of the booklet accompanying the CD. There is a picture of three standing soldiers. Do not look at this if driving.

Which soldier is the tallest?

Illustration 4

Before you answer, look again. Most people will choose the soldier at the top right as it appears tallest. The reason that it appears to be tallest is because of the decreasing vertical lines that comprise the background. Actually, all of the soldiers are the same size. One only appears to be larger than the others, and again, it only appears larger because of the background against which it appears. Our brain is tricked as it interprets the figure against the background. The background is altered such that it appears to be going off into the distance, thus making the soldier at the right appear larger.

Artists utilize this method to get depth in their landscape paintings and a dimensional view. Lawrence A. Averill, in *Introductory Psychology* (1949) said, "We are the victims of the peculiarities of illusion when we misinterpret what somebody is saying, or misread what somebody has written, or misjudge distance, time, direction, or sequence." He went on to say that it is important that individuals understand that "this liability to error through false interpretation of stimuli occurs."

Just as the eye can be tricked and the brain misinterprets the picture projected by the eye, our emotions can also be tricked when occurring events are displayed against different backgrounds. For example, a person grieving over the death of a loved one may become more upset with a flippant remark by a fellow worker or a minor fender bender. The background of the grief will shadow or "color" the interpretation of conversations, actions, and conflicting feelings that are presently surrounding that individual suffering a loss.

When a person is in emotional pain, all feelings resulting from perceptions are sharper and darker. If one is in love, most things are viewed as wonderful and rosy. Individuals have to be careful about ricochet emotions—the person's painful grief can bounce back with feelings of anger or an unexpected, aggressive behavior, unwarranted in most instances. Sometimes a long-held or a deeply hidden emotional memory or action can create dark moods and/or denial of what is going on regarding that person.

Losses, such as a lost job, a lost love, or the death of a loved one may be more apparent and thus understood by those individuals who are around that person. What is not apparent is the residue or the leftover emotional wreckage of severe illnesses, severe accidents, or violent and physical confrontations. Ordinary mishaps such as being late to a meeting or missing a bus, or spilling something on one's clothes take on a different focus and a deeper intensity. Those people who can bounce back from tragic events don't understand why others cannot. Again, the background against which the tragic event occurs is different—seen and felt differently.

Not all emotions are the result of the mind being tricked. Love has a mental beginning, but there are many factors that are interrelated. Love is a complex system of many other systems that are relevant. Love is something everyone talks about, love is experienced by most in varying degrees, and love is known to have many levels and different directions. However, the research on love is varied, with the behaviorists at odds with the romantics.

Just as the eye can be tricked in relaying information to the brain, a person's emotions can likewise be tricked or misled. Sometimes emotional reasoning tops rational logic or reason. For example, "She/He can't be bad because I love her/him, and I couldn't love a bad person," is an example of denial and emotional reasoning. People are constantly saying things like "she's in a bad mood," or "he's not on top of his game," or other comments that indicate they are aware that other factors are influencing that person's emotions or behaviors. What people can often see in other individual's lives, they are unable to see in their own.

Why do we wait until tomorrow to do what needs to be done today?

THE THINKING THAT TRAPS

This is the first of three chapters that will provide information to assist you, the reader, in changing your thinking, your feelings, and your actions. The earlier chapters were explanations about why many people see, think, believe, or act the way many individuals do. Much of the information was not personable. Information can be dull and sometimes skipped. It is difficult to involve individuals in a meaningful way. Some chapters lend themselves to a more personable presentation. While these last few chapters are written in the third person, try to become directly involved as the reader. Think "it's me" who must be involved and complete the assignments.

The three chapters are presented separately but all three work together as a system to help you initiate change. An individual needs to review these chapters and reflect on the suggestions, especially when he or she becomes disappointed or discouraged with the slowness of change. Remember, there may have been years utilized in setting up or building patterns of thoughts, reservoirs of feelings, and toolboxes of habitual behaviors. Even though thinking, feeling, and acting are presented in different chapters, each are dependent on the other two and work systematically to impact our lives.

This first chapter discusses thinking. Some people draw out a diagram on a piece of paper to visually depict the following descriptions. Some people who are auditory learners may only need to visualize it mentally. It would be helpful to later transfer the mental picture to a written one. The sequence of steps discussed in all three chapters is listed in the illustrations at the end of the book.

First, draw an equal-sided triangle, like a pyramid, half the size of a piece of notebook paper. Put a capital *T* on the lower left, outside corner of the triangle. Put a capital *F* on the lower right of the triangle, and a capital *A* at the top or tip of the triangle. Now draw arrows from *T* to *F* to *A* and back down to *T*. This illustrates that *T* leads to *F* which leads to *A* which in turn leads to *T*. This is a closed system.

Now, under *T* write *think* and under *F* write *feelings*. If thinking (*T*) leads to feelings (*F*) as indicated by the arrow, what word choice would be likely a result of thinking and feeling that would begin with an (*A*)? *Action* is the word. Thinking leads to feelings which lead to actions. However, actions reinforce the thinking and feelings so the arrow from (*A*) to (*F*) depicts this. A closed system in indicated.

The outside of the triangle is the present. The inside of the triangle is the past. One can understand that if one thinks sad thoughts, such as thinking of the loss of a loved one, then that thinking of a sad event can cause one to feel sad which in turn will cause one to cry or appear to be sad or may even prompt deliberate actions to try to forget the sadness. These actions could be constructive such as helping a charity or someone, or the actions could be destructive, such as drinking or drug use. The actions always impact the thoughts and feelings.

Some other examples are these: If one thinks angry, then one feels angry; and while observable actions may not be present, there are internal actions taking place. Remember, the anger (emotion) phase (F) does not skip the thinking phase. An explanation will follow later that will explain this. However, a lot of people would like to believe that they acted without thinking. That is almost impossible, although the thinking before the action may be in mini-seconds.

If a person thinks prejudice, jealousy, or happiness or love, how does one feel? And once the feelings are invoked, how does one act? Then those actions reinforce the thoughts and feelings. Thinking that there is no hope, no love, no way out of a deeply disturbing situation often leads to depressed thinking. This type of replay thinking may lead to feelings of depression and thoughts of suicide and deep feelings of despair. Fortunately, for most people, the thoughts and feelings do not ultimately result in the cycle completion in which action is taken. However, any talk of suicide or attempts should be taken seriously and professional help obtained. The deadly lure of a suicide action is that the person's very severe, depressed thinking and feelings are ended.

The above explanation provides some information about the *present* time of the system of thinking, feeling, acting, and feeling again. In the next chapter, an explanation of the impact of past thoughts, past feelings and past actions is given. Not every thought results in some type of action, but most thoughts invoke, although it may be hard to detect, some type of feeling. For example, when a person thinks the sunset is beautiful, there is a feeling of appreciation of nature and a feeling of satisfaction.

Finally, not all thinking, feeling, acting cycles are bad. Love, religious faith, friendships, and family are only a few of the good cycles. In the next chapter, the influence of the *past* is examined. The person must be well grounded in the concepts of the system that cycles in order to effect any desired change of behavior.

Why do we wait until tomorrow to do what needs to be done today?

FEELINGS TO ATTITUDES AND ACTIONS TO HABITS

You should remember, the interior of the T-F-A triangle is basically the past. The outside of the triangle is basically the present. However, the past intrudes into the present, and many times the present is held somewhat hostage by that past. Remember, this triangle is a closed system at this point, with the actions of the present reinforcing the thinking and feelings of the present. It needs some explanation that a closed system for human behavior can vary among individuals. Some people have an almost totally closed system while others have a mostly closed system.

The thinking of the present is rarely without impact from the past. Individuals draw on past experiences to attempt to understand what is happening in the present time and to try to make some prediction about the future. The experiences can be from firsthand knowledge, from the observation of others' experiences, and from insight obtained from reading, lectures, conversations, and media portrayals. For example, watching a boxing match is safer than watching a street fight, which is safer than actually being involved with a fistfight. Many individuals, including you, can still remember the emotional shock of the first truly scary horror movie. Few want to be a participant in a real-life horror drama.

Look at or remember the T-F-A triangle, with the arrows going from *thinking* to *feeling* to *actions*. If a feeling is held long enough, repeated enough, or felt deeply enough, that feeling usually becomes an attitude. For example, feelings of sadness, racism, arrogance, and many other attitudes can develop into attitudes that mold many actions without that person's awareness of why he or she is feeling that way. Good feelings such as love, empathy, sympathy, patience, and many others also develop into attitudes. Happy feelings develop into positive attitudes.

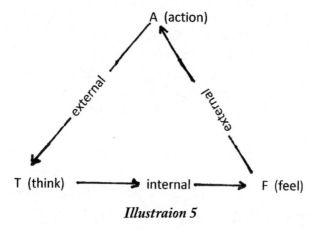

Illustraion 5

What is shown is that with repeated feelings developing into attitudes (that may govern our feelings) there is a direct impact on the actions that may follow such an attitude. A continued action becomes a habit. Just as continued feelings develop into attitudes, the attitudes funnel into repeated actions that in turn become habits. Most people would be shocked to discover how many of their feelings/attitudes and actions/habits focus their lives. There is little questioning of why they take the actions they take or believe the way they believe.

A number of writers and professional psychologists have discussed the impact of the early childhood years, the adolescent pressure-cooker years, and the cultural influences that shape many young adults. While it can be self-serving to say or believe that one can act without thinking of the consequences, that is somewhat rare. A rational human being always thinks before acting, most times with that thinking being bathed in a feeling. The thinking may be microseconds in length, but thinking takes place. Some people want to believe that "I was too angry" or "too drunk" or "too surprised" or "too scared" to be responsible for their actions. Comedian Skip Wilson used to say, "The devil made me do it." Being held accountable for one's actions is scary for some. When a person is told, "you are responsible for what you do," there is often denial.

Remember the impact that our mental filters have on selecting the response that eventually we show. Again, the above comments are general in nature for most people most of the time—for most people who are normal most of the time. The present is directed by the past more times than not, with such direction being unconscious most of the time. Repeated past emotions become imbedded attitudes, and repeated actions become ingrained habits. Again, a reminder for you: The arrow from the tip of the triangle, the *A* or the *action* (and now the *habit*) part of the system is directed back to the *T* or *thinking* portion of the triangle system.

Take anger for instance. If the person thinks he or she is deeply insulted, the resulting emotion may be anger; and if the insult has past experiences behind it, the attitude/current emotion goes to the action or habit part of the system. The person has habits of displaying intense anger such as cursing, yelling, hitting something, threatening, and a number of other anger-display methods. Clenching one's teeth or narrowing of the eyes and other more subtle forms of anger expression may be shown. However, all of these actions reinforce the thinking that was the original cause, which feeds the emotion, and more actions or more intensity of an action is a result that moves again to reinforce the thinking.

Most intense emotions cannot be sustained indefinitely, although rethinking of a past event can bring back repressed emotions. Likewise, intense actions, even though those actions may be habitual, eventually may extinguish before real damage is done to relationships or to property. Intense emotions and resultant unacceptable behaviors do occur for some people. Sometimes normal people temporarily do abnormal things.

A partial review of the T-F-A triangle is warranted. If a person has drawn a triangle and placed *thinking* at the left side, *feeling* on the right side of the triangle, and *actions* at the peak of the triangle, the next step is adding *past thoughts/memories* below thinking, *attitudes* below feelings, and *habits/memories* above actions. The arrows remain the same. Remember, the interior of the triangle is the past—the past thoughts and experiences, the past feelings, and the past actions. The outside of the triangle is the present.

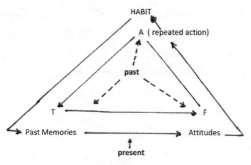

Illustraion 6

You should understand that the above explanations are really simplified, generalized, and evolve from beliefs of the writer who utilized this method of explanation and subsequent therapy to initiate a change in the thinking, feelings, and behaviors of his clients. In the next chapter, a method to change and disengage the T-F-A closed system is discussed. Keep the diagram for additional elements to be added to it in order to visually outline the expected sequence of evolved thinking and then the desired change.

This too-brief explanation as to why and when individuals do what they do may confuse individuals more than help them. However, a general understanding of the preceding two chapters and an acceptance of most of those explanations is needed before tackling the next chapter which deals with a method to change the systematic cycle in the future context.

As with most successful life changes, there is a reason and need to change. That change is based on information and steps regarding methods utilized to change, and a willingness to engage in those behaviors to be changed. There has to be support and encouragement while implementing the desired change, and almost all individuals need external validation of the improvement of the desired behavioral change. Commitment, practice, follow-through, and some type of reward for success are also key ingredients. Many diet plans fail because these key ingredients are not followed, and many New Year's resolutions meet a similar fate.

Why do we wait until tomorrow to do what needs to be done today?

CHANGING THE BEHAVIOR

Almost all of the preceding chapters have been developed to this most important chapter. If a person truly wants to change his or her behavior, this chapter provides one method to do so. In the preceding two chapters, the explanation was drafted about the T-F-A triangle. In review, the *T* stood for *thinking*, the *F* stood for *feelings* and *A* stood for *actions* and the arrows went from *T* to *F* to *A* back to *T*. In most instances, this is a closed system and indicates the past. As time passes, the past thoughts influence the present thinking, the past feelings become attitudes, and the past actions become habits.

Remember that past thoughts are written under the *T*, attitudes are written under the *F*, and habits are written above the *A*. The past thoughts, the attitudes and the habits are all part of the present. In addition, the present includes the current thinking. If the triangle diagram is being used, write in all of these designations or points. The arrows have been used to illustrate these main points: (1) thinking leads to feelings which lead to actions which lead to reinforcing the thinking which emphasizes the feelings which in turn stimulates the continued action, (2) this progression and cycle can produce attitudes and habits, both of which may direct a person's life without that person being aware of it.

Think of the many unconscious habits that people use in their daily lives. When a person bends over to pick up something from the ground, that person doesn't think, *Which hand should I use?*. Typically, the right-handed person will pick up the item with his or her right hand. If a person decided to tie a shoe in a hurry, that person doesn't have to think, *How do I tie a shoe?* From shaving, to putting on lipstick, to smiling at a cute baby's picture, to typing, or texting on a cell phone and many other daily activities, these habits enable individuals to efficiently use their time.

Sometimes the problem is that habits can also be a drain on one's emotions and can cause an individual to feel that he or she is not in control of the behavior or feelings that the individual is utilizing. The cycle reinforces the habit. Smoking is a habit that many can quit by utilizing the strategy in this chapter. An individual who is using illegal drugs almost always has to have professional help. A person who is unfriendly can be helped by this chapter, but a person who has severe depression will also need professional help. Temporary bouts of feeling low may be helped by this chapter's strategy.

Habits are established by repeated actions. Some experts believe that an action that is repeated in a similar fashion 27 to 37 times will become a habit. Most habits are continually being reinforced by repetition and are beneficial to a successful and happy life. Some habits are not good for the individual and limit and hurt the individual in a number of ways. For a bad habit, the past and current thinking and the attitudes that have emerged from constantly feeling a certain way reinforce the habitual way of behaving. Unfortunately, it is easier to establish a habit than it is to break or change the habit.

Some psychologists believe that a patient must change his or her thoughts and feelings first before attempting to change the behavior. In this chapter, the emphasis is on changing the behavior and subsequently, changes in the thinking and feelings will follow. Remember the arrows that led from *T* to *F* to *A* to *T* and then continue to *F* to *A* to *T* and so on? Those arrows are designed to indicate that the motion of the cycle— the direction and emphasis of the cycle—follows the sequence of those arrows. The question becomes, *How does one break the cycle?*

An individual breaks the cycle by acting differently than he or she is thinking or feeling. The individual must act differently, and change the habitual act that has been reinforced by the attitude(s) that created the repetitive act in the first place. A person will have difficulty if told to think a certain way or to feel a certain way, but if told to do an observable behavior, such as "hold up your hand" or "lick your lips" or "shake hands" or even "smile," most can do it. An individual does have control over most of his or her developed behaviors.

Look at the T-F-A triangles in the preceding chapter. If an individual were to draw a line, left to right, halfway between the *A* at the top of the triangle and the *T* and *F* at the bottom of the triangle, the arrow from the *A* (or *action*) and the *habit* top of the triangle, the arrow from the *A* to the *T* is intersected or stopped. The line should be drawn past the left one side of the triangle. This line, a horizon type of line that is goes past the other side of the triangle, is designed to show that stopping the habitual action stops the replenishing of the thinking and feelings/emotions and attitudes that in turn stimulate and reinforce the action(s) that have become a habit.

Behavior Changed

action/habit

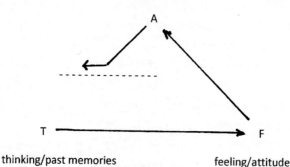

thinking/past memories   feeling/attitude

No Reinforcement

Illustraion 7

Simply put, an individual must *act differently* than he or she *thinks* or *feels*. The new *future action* or the avoidance of an old *(bad) action/habit* does not stimulate the current or past/present thinking and feelings/attitudes. The difficulty is while repeated actions may become habits after 27 to 37 repetitions, undoing a habit may require some 60 to 125 repeated avoidances or failures to undo the bad habit. A smoker may have to place gum in his or her mouth instead of a cigarette many dozens and dozens of times to extinguish the bad habit by replacement with a better alternate action.

Because this change action concept is simple, it can be very difficult to do. People with racial attitudes have been successful in replacing prejudicial attitudes with tolerance by acting differently from the older learned attitudes and habits. The thoughts and feelings change more slowly than positive actions. It is the actions/habits that control the thoughts and feelings and attitudes. Changing or stopping the action/habit, diminishes the intensity of the thinking and feeling process.

It should be understood that the longer a habit or an attitude has been done or held, the more difficult it is to change it. A belief is a combination of past thinking, past experiences, past environments, past parental (or some significant adult[s] during childhood) guidance, past emotional engagements, and past and current social morals. A belief is a stepchild of thinking and feeling. However, even most beliefs have to have actions to sustain their continuance.

There are several reasons why this simple method to change undesired behavior(s) will not work:

(1) Many people feel most comfortable believing that others are responsible for their behavior. "My dad had a bad temper," "Our family has always...," "When I'm drunk I...," "I was bullied," "The color of my skin has...," "I'm from the poor side of the tracks," "I didn't have any...," "I was a drug baby," "I had this illness (or accident) that...," and many other excuses. What cannot be challenged is that many successful individuals have had those same environmental or background excuses or reasons or limitations, but they became successful anyway.

(2) In this day of instant medication to make a person feel better, sleep longer, enjoy a more satisfying sexual relationship, and with commercials promising a more beautiful skin or hair instantly, there is a tendency to seek some external or medical means to effectively change one's undesirable behavior. There are a wide variety of entertainment and athletic games to entertain and encourage one to put off changing any behavior. Some individuals do not want to take the time or the responsibility for change. "Someone else should do this for me," or "I need someone to tell me exactly how to do what I want to do, when I want to do it, at no cost, and at my convenience." Sadly, life is not like that.

(3) Individuals may not understand the dynamics to the triangle and may not believe in the cycle and the method to break undesired habits. As Abigail Van Buren said, "A bad habit never disappears miraculously; it's an 'undo-it-yourself' project."

(4) Individuals fail to consistently and faithfully follow the practice of doing a different but better action in order to extinguish the old undesired action/behavior. "When patterns are broken, new worlds can emerge," said Tuli Kupferberg.

When a person has developed a perceptual awareness, is honest with himself, is genuine in wanting to improve himself, is willing to initiate the needed changes in a systematic manner by following and practicing, again and again, the examples given throughout the book, then that person can be successful in making improvements in his life.

An individual needs to realize that change and improvement come in slow increments, over a period of time. For most people, there are few "jumps" or improvement "gains" within a couple of weeks. What is readily apparent to most is the difference between how they now believe, feel, and behave and how they could believe, feel, and behave. And finally, individuals need to be patient and to take pride in small accomplishments. The *most important* suggestion of all is to review the relevant chapters in this book and reflect on the interrelated systems of life.

Why do we wait until tomorrow to do what needs to be done today?

SADDEST OF WORDS

It should be understood by now that the main purpose of this book is to indicate to the reader that the key to self-improvement lies in taking action, immediately. Too many individuals put off the needed improvement, and tomorrow is put off until the next tomorrow, and the next, until finally, a year of remaining the same has passed. The original desire for self-improvement is diminished by the chains of habit.

The near-concluding lines of the poem titled *Maud Muller*, by John Greenleaf Whittier, are appropriate for the concluding segment of this book. The significant two lines of this poem are:

> Of all the sad words
> Of tongue or pen,
> The saddest are these,
> 'What might have been.'

It should be noted that "what might have been" was at one time a "what could be" goal in a young individual's dream. It may have become an impossible dream for some older individuals who have given up. There are others who may pass on this type of negative thinking to others. Because the young do not believe that dream obtainment is unrealistic, many are able to obtain the goals of their dreams. Yet, many fail because they lack persistence or confidence, or because the journey is hard and time-consuming. However, most individuals fail because they do not believe in themselves enough to begin. Unless effort is begun and maintained, nothing can be accomplished.

To interject a personal note, this book would not be available if an earlier dream of college had not begun. For me, a "what could be" dream in the early 1960s became then an accomplishment, a "what was" in later life. This book could have become a discarded dream in a dusty memory box that, in my retirement years, would have been regretfully remembered as a "might have been."

For many people, improving one's behavior or attitude is as difficult as the writing of a book. What is most sad is that so many do not even make the attempt to improve themselves, although much verbiage to do so is given. It is similar to an overweight person saying "I need to go on a diet" as he or she accepts a third helping of food. The thought that one must do, or will do what is needed, at a later time is comforting.

There is even a sense of satisfaction in the words "I failed" that is not available with the words "I didn't try." There are many sad words in all languages, but in any language, in any country, and in any period of time in civilization, the *saddest of words* continue to be "what might have been." This book is just the beginning, the "what could be." After reading it, each individual must decide for himself if his life is to be "what can be," or will it become "what might have been!" "Might have been" are truly the saddest of words.

Why do we wait until tomorrow to do what needs to be done today?

AFTERWORD

We can be prisoners of our beliefs and be comfortable with those beliefs. We have our habitual behaviors that form predictable and worry-free systems and cycles, many of which have developed from years of the same patterns of thinking. To change one's eating habits, even though the need is a medical necessity, and begin to go on the required diet is extremely difficult. It is even more difficult to change one's perceptions about oneself and others.

The chapters discuss the need to develop an awareness of one's thinking, an awareness of how one's feelings are developed from one's thinking, and how both the thinking and the feeling are reinforced by the behaviors. Among the various divisions of psychological orientation is one that utilizes how to treat an individual's emotional problem. The earlier view was that a therapist had to change the thoughts and feelings in order to change the behavior. This is a much longer process. The behaviorists think that the therapist should change the behavior(s) or work on changing the behaviors which in turn will change the thoughts and feelings.

There is really no simple answer to changing a person's behavior, no quick method to change what needs to be changed, and no guarantee that the change will remain permanent, as life is too fluid and involves too many people facing unknown situations to have certainty. It should be noted that while the writer believes that habits direct our lives and that we can change those habits, it was H. L. Mencken who said, "For every human problem, there is a neat, simple solution, and it is always wrong."

This writer believes that behaviors must be changed first. It makes sense that one can control his behaviors easier than he can control his thoughts and feelings. There has to be a belief that a person is in control of his life (internal locus of control). When asked to raise his arm, the person can do so, if he so desires to follow the request. If asked to feel very happy or asked to think about pink elephants, the person may not be able to comply.

The next to last three chapters provide the method to change one's undesired habit(s) by changing how one acts or behaves, i.e., acting differently than what one feels and thinks. If a person thinks of something that makes him feel sad, he should act happy. By putting a smile on his face, greeting people cheerfully, doing some positive things for other people, and other tasks that is usually done when he is happy, he begins to derail the thinking-feeling-acting cycle that reinforces a system. Bottom line, we can control most of our behaviors. Medical problems, serious mental or emotional problems, and drug dependency problems are the exception.

A major problem is the modern belief that we cannot solve our own problems. This belief is reinforced by magazine articles, TV shows, commercials, and some professionals. Friends can help, but the individual being helped must have the need or desire, the persistence and patience to follow through, and the belief that he can improve or change his life. Remember that these changes are usually smaller adjustments, a minor tune-up and not a major overhaul.

There were some college experiments where the students were told to make an angry face and to hold on the clenched jaw and narrowed eyes for a period of five minutes or longer. The students reported that they begin to feel angry, and the longer the physical behavior of being angry was maintained, the more angry they became.

It is reasonable to assume that if behaviors can make one angry, then utilizing happy behaviors or actions would change the feeling of sadness. For many people, continuing to do the behavior that is opposite the feeling will usually diminish the intensity of the feeling and weaken the thinking that caused or accompanying the feeling. It takes only fifteen muscles to smile, but it takes forty-five muscles to frown. Research has shown that when facial muscles are trained, such as having a constant frown, the training will cause the facial muscles to "set." If a person is constantly smiling, the "smile muscles" get set and his thinking, his attitude, his feelings, and his resultant behaviors are usually shown as being happy as well.

One of the first rules of perception is that no person devotes effort to proving himself wrong, and a humorous second rule of perception is that the person who can smile when things go wrong has thought of someone on whom to blame the mishap.

John Gardner, in his book titled *Excellence*, talks of one way of measuring excellence that uses comparisons between people—some run faster or are better musicians. There are card games, athletic contests, race cars, ironman contests, game shows, and many, many other ways that there is an apparent comparison or a measurement against a standard or record compared to others. He indicated that another comparison is between an individual—that comparison is between that individual at his best and that same individual at his worst.

Famous author Norman Vincent Peale was quoted as saying, "You are the CEO of how you are doing and where you are going." A person shouldn't let the bad-day syndrome get management of his life. If a person says "I'm going to have a good day," that person with that attitude will have a ninety percent chance of actually having that day be a good day. A person should not complain to others. For one thing, no one likes to be around a complainer. An unknown source of humor which may have a factual basis is that eighty percent of the people don't care if the complainer has problems, and some twenty percent are glad that the complainer does have problems.

For many people, the right answer is "the one we believe in." The right answer for them is not always the correct answer and it may not be the answer that the majority of people believe is right or correct. Not examining the answer "we believe in" is a type of mental quicksand. Such a belief will trap an individual and sink him. New research, new discoveries, new challenges, and new opportunities are not examined by the individual who is caught up in the mental quicksand.

A quotation by Oliver Wendell Holmes Sr. is important to remember. He said, "A man's mind, stretched by a new idea, can never go back to its original dimension." Hopefully, this book has stretched your knowledge, has provided some insight as to people's behaviors, and given some encouragement and methods to change the systematic cycle of undesired behavioral habits.

Really, why do we wait until tomorrow to do what needs to be done today?

INDEX OF ILLUSTRATIONS/ DIAGRAMS